D1297574

World without Heroes

World without Heroes

The Brooklyn Novels of Daniel Fuchs

Marcelline Krafchick

Rutherford • Madison • Teaneck
Fairleigh Dickinson University Press
London and Toronto: Associated University Presses

© 1988 by Associated University Presses, Inc.

Associated University Presses
440 Forsgate Drive
Cranbury, NJ 08512

Associated University Presses
25 Sicilian Avenue
London WC1A 2QH, England

Associated University Presses
P.O. Box 488, Port Credit
Mississauga, Ontario
Canada L5G 4M2

The paper used in this publication meets the requirements
of the American National Standard for Permanence of Paper
for Printed Library Materials Z39.48-1984.

Library of Congress Cataloging-in-Publication Data

Krafchick, Marcelline.
    World without heroes.

    Bibliography: p.
    Includes index.
    1. Fuchs, Daniel, 1909–   —Criticism and
interpretation.   I. Title.
PS3511.U27Z75   1988   813'.52   86-46339
ISBN 0-8386-3312-9 (alk. paper)

PRINTED IN THE UNITED STATES OF AMERICA

Contents

For Toby
(Mervyn Tobias, 1911–1986)

Acknowledgments

I am grateful to John Updike, who suggested that I write about Daniel Fuchs's fiction when I had not read a word of it. I am indebted to Peter Hays and Karl Zender, whose good will and tough criticism carried me through the project. Many thanks, finally, to Daniel Fuchs, for being accessible and good-humored, for showing more interest in my career than in his, and for reminding me not to take things too seriously. His sentences, even in a note dashed off on yellow scratch paper, continue to strike me as magical.

World without Heroes

1
Introduction

The present resurgence of interest in American literature of the 1930s can be expected, like the renewed attention to that decade during the sixties, to adjust some reputations. One writer of the thirties, novelist Daniel Fuchs, has up to this time largely been dismissed from discussions of the period with distinct but brief praise. The task of this study is to examine Fuchs's neglected literary merits. The resistance of his writing to conventional categories may in part account for the dearth of investigations into those merits. For that reason the task of this chapter is to consider his work in relation to its critical context.[1]

Although Fuchs has published four novels and over fifty short stories, sixteen of them in *The New Yorker,* his literary reputation, such as it is, rests mainly on three novels he wrote in the 1930s, *Summer in Williamsburg* (1934), *Homage to Blenholt* (1936), and *Low Company* (1937). While reviews of the novels were favorable on the whole, they were, in Fuchs's words, scanty and immaterial, and the three novels together sold only about two thousand copies.[2] Reissued as *Three Novels* in 1961, they again met with enthusiastic but unsustained interest. The paperback edition of the three novels combined as *The Williamsburg Trilogy* in 1971 was greeted as well by praise from a few critics and soon went out of print.[3]

Because the Brooklyn novels deal with the harshness of urban life in the thirties, Fuchs has been regarded as a social novelist, and in part he is. Because he uses a Jewish context for his first two novels, he has been labeled a Jewish-American writer, and in part he is. But readers who have concentrated on his gift for mimesis of city life have tended to find him wanting either as social or Jewish novelist. His strength, in fact, which has appeared to be a weakness, is the importing of philosophical questioning and modernist techniques into the apparently proletarian novel. The focus in this study will be on examining the means by which Fuchs challenges both social and artistic certainties.

"Nobody else writes like Daniel Fuchs," according to John Updike.[4] Commentators associate Fuchs's work with that of such disparate authors as Hemingway, Dostoevsky, Bellow, Farrell, Faulkner, and Chekhov; Stanley Edgar Hyman places him with the "symbolists and fantasists" Nathanael West and Henry Roth.[5] His ties with other writers, as this chapter should demonstrate, are in no instance strong enough to establish him in a movement or school of writing. Regarded by contemporaries like Irving Howe as insufficiently political, especially for a Jewish writer from Brooklyn during the Depression, he is not part of the proletarian movement that dominates the urban literature produced in that decade. And though his gangster material and pacing may put him close to the tough-guy school, he does not associate violence with a heroic figure; the presence of a hero is incompatible with Fuchs's synthesis of competing viewpoints.

The immense sales of the decade's most popular novels show the public taste for escape, to China in Pearl Buck's *The Good Earth,* Napoleonic Europe in Hervey Allen's *Anthony Adverse,* and the Civil War South in Margaret Mitchell's *Gone With the Wind.* But a preponderance of serious artists and critics in the thirties, particularly urban writers, were committed to abolishing social wrongs through the rise of the working class, the issue among them being not whether to be revolutionary, but how revolutionary to become; such terms of the period as "liberal-radicals" and "quasi-Trotskyist" evoke these shadings. James T. Farrell writes that only a few writers were, like Faulkner, uninvolved in the "politicoliterary debates" which dominated both literature and criticism in the decade.[6] In this period, as historian Daniel Aaron remarks with irony, leading critics "constantly reminded writers still hanging in the liberal limbo between communism and capitalism that Marxism was not only morally uplifting and . . . intellectually clarifying but that it also made better artists. Prose style, after all, was intimately related to the writer's comprehension of the world around him."[7] Granville Hicks, one of the most influential believers that "there is no such thing as neutrality," argued that "the discovery of the class struggle as the fundamental interpretation of American life presents [the] problem to the artists of his own position in the conflict."[8]

Readers who are accustomed to focusing on the autonomous text may disdain the ardent social realists of the thirties as naive and misguided, but in 1930 the damage done by the economic system was compellingly evident, and many artists (not only writers) saw themselves as occupants of a sinking ship, for whom the need to bail water preempted the luxury of a private vision or exploring of nuances. As the decade advanced, a burgeoning *esprit de corps* obliged these artists to display their courage to undo the breakdown of basic life—it was not enough to have a gift. Edmund Wilson, the decade's finest critic, observed later that during the thirties many writers either stopped writing or compromised their beliefs. Shortly after Daniel Fuchs moved to Hollywood to write films, the literary scene became more tolerant, but the damage done to him and others by the lapse in artistic disinterestedness had been considerable. Wilson himself, warmed to anticapitalism by the Sacco and Vanzetti executions in 1927 and a communist supporter after his research for a chronicle of Depression America,[9] cited after his disenchantment a fundamental error of radical thirties criticism which had affected the careers of individualistic writers like Fuchs: "the assumption that great novels and plays must necessarily be written by people who have everything clear in their minds."[10] In his assessment of the decade Howe writes, "The truth is that the bulk of left-wing literary criticism was marked by an inquisitorial narrowness of spirit."[11] Ironically, Howe's own application of such narrowness to Fuchs's fiction may have helped to keep Fuchs one of the era's casualties.[12]

Period and genre classifications, the necessary evils of literary discussion, leave an individualistic writer like Fuchs without a niche. One category that impedes a fair reading of his novels is what David Madden calls "our mythical Thirties."[13] Donald Pizer, in attempting to rescue Farrell from the stereotype of that era, looks at the strengths that *Studs Lonigan* gains from both the twenties and the thirties. His remarks might apply as well to Fuchs's work. Pizer characterizes the twenties by "the dramatization of the inarticulate felt life . . . [as it] interacts with a social reality that informs and often collides with it," and the thirties by depression subject matter, documentary method, and an emphasis on tragic waste and misdirection.[14] Fuchs, like Farrell, depends less on Depression subject matter than on the tragic waste produced by the collision of the inarticulate felt life with social reality.

Farrell himself observed about the thirties that, apart from such writers as Fuchs and Henry Roth, who he believed had genuine value, the decade was rife with less important fiction than the twenties, and was characterized by such "hard-boiled" works as Steinbeck's *Of Mice and Men* and James M. Cain's *The Postman Always Rings Twice*.[15] Edmund Wilson, too, preferred the writing of the twenties, before writers became preoccupied "with making sure their positions were correct in relation to the capitalist system."[16] This controlling expectation in literary criticism is exemplified in a review of *Low Company* by Albert Halper, a novelist writing at the same time as Fuchs whose own proletarian message reduces his characters to stereotypes. Because all the characters and their tragedies in *Low Company* are petty, Halper writes, and they are all frustrated in their efforts, even "pages and pages of superb writing" are able to take the book "nowhere." Halper is troubled by Fuchs's lack of a "place to lay down his burden," of an ordering perception that would lend purpose to frustration. That exigent purpose found wanting, Halper is left without a set of aesthetic terms to account for his finding the novel "queerly powerful, disturbing."[17]

Among the distinguished American writers in the thirties, including Faulkner, Fitzgerald, and Hemingway, it is Steinbeck who most directly places the documenting of Depression hardship at the foreground of his work. Still, it is difficult in the works of other authors in this group, in *Tender is the Night,* for example, to separate personal from social consciousness. These writers often use an outcast or group of outcasts as hero to convey a rejection of modern values that had begun before the Depression. Hyman, in his attempt to characterize the thirties period, praises West's *Miss Lonelyhearts* (1933) for elements it shares with the twenties novels that he regards as the finest of the century, *The Great Gatsby* and *The Sun Also Rises;* these elements, according to Hyman, are "a lost and victimized hero, a bitter sense of our civilization's falsity, a pervasive melancholy atmosphere of failure and defeat."[18] Fuchs's novels convey a similar sense of falsity and defeat, yet he denies the reader the escape of identifying with "a lost and victimized hero."

That absence of a hero removes Fuchs from another classification of writing with which he has elements in common, the tough-guy school that flourished in the thirties, Edmund Wilson's "Boys in the Back Room,"[19] who included such writers as Dashiell Hammett, Raymond Chandler, James M. Cain, John O'Hara, and Horace McCoy. The tough-guy genre, usually novella-length and associated with urban Los Angeles rather than Chicago or New York, began for the most part with stories in the magazine *Black Mask* as an offshoot of the hard-boiled detective story. The genre is characterized by an emphasis on plot, the exposure of corruption being incidental to the telling of a stark, dynamic, unsentimentally violent story.

Fuchs's writing resembles the tough school, as David Madden calls it,[20] in the absence of ideology and the dispassionate portrayal of violence. Although many of the genre's writers, like Hammett, were actively or sympathetically leftist in private life, and they regularly depict the hypocrisy of the gentry as the cause of social disorder, their attention to plot overshadows any ideological intent. The neutral treatment of violence, which Fuchs also shares with the tough school, is evident in other serious writers, for example Faulkner in *Sanctuary*, Steinbeck in *Of Mice and Men,* and Hemingway in *To Have and Have Not.* But despite these dignifying ties, the genre itself has largely become an artifact of the decade's search for thrills and simplification, in the view of Alfred Kazin a transformation of Hemingway's nihilism into titillation.[21] Fuchs's casual use of violence has nothing to do with the commercializing of gratuitous sensation.

Tough-guy stories, though purportedly realistic, are often told in first person by a narrator who is too self-absorbed, as in Cain's *The Butterfly,* for example, to introduce the array of observations that might make the setting palpable. And the writers in this genre, although conspicuously rebellious against romanticism with their hardened attitude toward brutality, are in fact romantic in supporting, like Hemingway, the mystique of the sexually attractive renegade hero.

Fuchs introduces beatings and killing in his novels casually and graphically, and in his third novel integrates these into a tightly paced plot, but he is unlike the tough-guy group in several respects that are useful in discussing him. David Madden writes of James M. Cain that "most of [his] heroes are self-seeking, antigroup, anticommunity," and that Cain's interest is in his hero's "relation to himself or to the woman he loves."[22] The emphasis on a hero conveyed in this passage is alien to Fuchs's conception, as is the notion that relation to oneself or one's beloved (for example, Philip Hayman's to himself and Ruth) can be independent of community. The tough-guy writers responded to the decade's American dream-turned-nightmare in terms of the mystique of virility. Fuchs, instead, mocks the tough stance in a number of his characterizations, such as the surly-veneered street youths, Davey and Natie the Buller, in *Summer in Williamsburg,* the blustering Shorty in *Low Company,* and the aimless and dependent henchmen in all three works.

The two most essential distinctions between the work of Fuchs and the tough school, however, are also the most illuminating about him. The first is that Fuchs tempers his cynicism with a tenderness that occasionally leads to lyricism in his portraits. The second is that, despite the tough novel's obligatory protagonist and frequent use of a first-person narrator, and despite its attention to the hero's relation to himself on some level, it is not a novel of character, and character is Fuchs's primary concern.

Because of his Jewish background and his use of mostly Jewish characters in his first two novels, and perhaps also because he was not a proletarian reformist, some critics have assigned Fuchs to the niche of American-Jewish novelist. Irving Howe calls him "Jewish to the marrow,"[23] on the basis of Fuchs's mocking stoicism and mindfulness of the essential sadness of things. Irwin Shaw writes that in Fuchs's two novels set in Jewish households he is a literary father for Bellow, Malamud, and Roth, and David Madden calls Fuchs the progenitor of "a whole school of Jewish-American writing, from Odets to Roth."[24] Such paternity notwithstanding, and regardless of which among the inexhaustible definitions of Jewishness may be the most cogent,[25] critics have begun to recognize that the term can be as inappropriately limiting for American writers as is the regional designation in discussions of Faulkner and Anderson.[26]

Such critics as Morris Dickstein who have assigned Fuchs to the category of Jewish-American writer have made that category their basis for finding fault with his work. Dickstein writes in *Partisan Review* in 1974 that Fuchs is "notably ham-handed in portraying the religious life of the Jews, a more inward subject [than social history]."[27] In fact, Fuchs devotes very little attention to religious life. The confining label, whether ethnic or religious, hinders a just appraisal of the third novel especially. Most of its characters, like Shorty and Madame Pavlovna, are not meant to be even assimilated Jews, and others, like Herbert Lurie and Shubunka, are never identified as Jews. Readers who stress Fuchs's realistic portrayal of Jewish tenement life, while deploring the absence of ideological content, disregard such questions as why a mere social historian would omit the Dodgers from conversations in a Brooklyn summer, give his main character no first name, and create a fictitious name for his recognizable setting.

There is in fact not much more reason to designate *Low Company* than there is to label *Death of a Salesman* as Jewish-American literature. The inappropriateness of this designation for Fuchs's third novel is no doubt the reason why discussions that connect its author with Jewish writing usually disregard it, as if it had not been written.[28] Replying to a question about his Jewishness as a writer, Fuchs, who was born in this country, recently wrote, "It never occurred to me in my simplicity that I was not a member of the planet."[29] As in a number of Arthur Miller's plays, in which that

Jewish-American writer launders out his ethnic heritage, Fuchs in *Low Company* omits an ethnic context in order to expand the story's applicability, not merely to Americanize it but to universalize it.[30]

Vital shifts in treatment in the third novel are obscured by the usual lumping of the three novels together as a trilogy.[31] In *Low Company* Fuchs retains the impeccable fidelity to observation that leads Howe to describe him as a "pure" novelist, one who believes "in the sufficiency of rendering."[32] But Fuchs goes beyond mimesis to create the atmosphere of a modern fable. The setting in his third novel is not a household, Jewish or otherwise, but a garish ice-cream parlor that offers consoling sweets to bored beachgoers and serves as ironic surrogate home for the story's circle of vulnerable and self-seeking personalities. The two families represented in the novel have disintegrated, and the marriage which is imminent through most of the story is finally cancelled. All of the characters, including the few who are married, live essentially alone, and the absence of children, who play such an important part in the first two novels, is compatible with the novel's atmosphere of sterility, the absence of a future.

In *Low Company* Fuchs shifts from the family as world to the world as family. The characters are an interdependent community of emotional grotesques, in Anderson's sense of monomaniacs, viewed as if in the funhouse distorting mirror. They live in an imaginary version of a beach town where no one ever looks at the ocean, and where newspapers exist to report only racing odds and the death of one of the characters.

Fuchs's broad social concerns are evident in his emphasis both on the particular ugliness of Neptune Beach (and of Ann's ice-cream parlor) and on universal selfishness. But, free of the tendentious writer's need to divide the world into heroes and villains, Fuchs approaches his subjects with tolerant humor. In the bleak amusement community of *Low Company,* where human lives are desperately contingent on one another, two characters manage to touch each other with compassion hard-won. That is the apparent extent of Fuchs's message. Trusting only this fellow feeling as an absolute value, he declines to assign blame.

Blame was of course commonly directed in the thirties toward economic conditions, but while the Brooklyn novels are set in the midst of the Depression, they do not, according to Harvey Swados, "deal with the depression as such."[33] Swados is correct; Fuchs subdues the traditional elements present in stories of the Depression. There are no breadlines or evictions, and Mr. Hayman's regular Sunday excursion, in *Summer in Williamsburg,* for an extravagant breakfast of delicacies from smoked sturgeon to cheesecake shows the family's comfortable level of survival. In *Low Company* two of the three most miserable characters are wealthy.

Significantly, in all three novels employment appears to be a matter of choice. Even Arthur in *Low Company,* who has lost a job in Massachusetts, has found work as the dishwasher at Ann's. What keeps Fuchs's young Williamsburg men from working is the demeaning sameness and deadly anonymity of available jobs, rather than a shortage of them.

For Fuchs, whatever else the Depression may have been, including a metaphor for the conditions of urban industrialized humanity, it was primarily an exacerbation of the proletarian miseries the new country had to offer. Federal programs like Social Security have been responses since the thirties to an explosion of conditions that had existed before the country's economic collapse. Well before 1929 the immigrant culture faced many of the problems that are associated with the Depression. For many, the Depression began whenever they arrived to find themselves peddling from pushcarts or working sixteen hours or longer each day in airless, poorly lit, and patently hazardous factories.

The breakdown of community among the displaced immigrants, and the loss of physical space—recalled in Mrs. Balkan's reverie, in *Homage to Blenholt,* of running through fields of flowers—are shown to have soured the spirit as much as did the dearth of incomes; the incomes themselves may have been greater than in the old country. Worst of all, the prospect of drudging insignificance is what horrifies Harry and Philip Hayman in *Summer in Williamsburg* and lends crime its attractiveness as an alternative. That prospect, too, is what invites Max Balkan and Mendel Munves, in *Homage to Blenholt,* to attach romance to the ownership of a delicatessen store. As an entrepreneur, Max can dream of a chain of stores extending to San Francisco, and Munves can imagine a salon "for tea and talk."

The Depression, then, is a symptom for Fuchs of a profound illness that preceded it historically. The glamorous opportunities that tantalize through billboards, movies, and the rotogravure attract the clever, like Papravel, and the talentless, like Rita Balkan, to dream of testing their abilities in the American arena, where spunk and chance rule. If, as Label Balkan tells us, America is "ganev" or thieving land, his son's capacity to imagine is a priceless commodity, and in the society in which the Balkans live, that imaginative faculty has value only if it makes Max a living. Fuchs's gamblers, criminals, and dreamers alike can look around at the instant aristocracy that arrives through luck and ingenuity rather than inheritance and ask, "Why not me?" For most of them there is no more important question.

This portrayal of America expands the social concerns of Fuchs's fiction beyond the decade in which he wrote. While in *Summer in Williamsburg* the wealthy Rubin's exploitation of immigrants in sweatshops reminds the reader of specific social abuses, Spitzbergen in *Low Company*, who is nearly deranged over money, is in an ahistoric tradition of misers that assumes a bitter dimension in the New World. The problem Fuchs expresses is deeper and older than the Depression:

> Even though [Mr. Hayman] has been in this country almost fifty years he disapproves of it, often with strong feeling, or heartfelt indignation. So many times Philip has heard him. . . , noting some unpleasant condition, protest, "miserable! It shouldn't be!" He says that there is no friendship, no brotherhood, no genuine feeling, pity, or charity.[34]

Mr. Hayman tells his son that in the old country "it was like a religious law to be merry and glad," but "everybody here makes a living, and there is no rest or quiet" (243). The substitution of commercial for humane values receives more attention from Fuchs than the crisis associated with the thirties.

It is not surprising, then, that, though Fuchs was writing in an era when many writers—including Michael Gold, Nelson Algren, Edward Dahlberg, and Richard Wright—were subscribing to a political program to rescue America, his novels reflect an uneasiness with doctrinaire solutions. Too skeptical for the pungency and rage that have gained Nathanael West a following, Fuchs displays the courage of ambivalence.

Philip Rahv remarks about the thirties that "the suffering imposed on the bulk of the population by the economic crisis elevated the 'common man' to a martyrdom that almost overnight integrated him into the sympathies of the literary artist."[35] But Fuchs was no more inclined to revolutionary optimism about his "low company" than he was to picturing them as determined by abstract agents. He approaches, only with ambiguity, the very same material that proletarian writing treats—buildings and pavements cracked, the smell of vinegar in tenement hallways, dead cats in the yard, domestic uproar, desperation. That ambiguity is expressed by the application of modernist methods to these nonmodernist subjects.

Fuchs's reluctance in his narratives to account for the sources of corruption, waste, and meanness is matched by a diffidence in his technique. He gives a design to indeterminacy by investing partial credibility in all his characters and withholding complete credibility from any single voice. With this aversion to an authoritative aspect he reflects the modernist paradox of conveying at the same time a position and a question about ultimates.

The Brooklyn novels are at the intersection of social and modernist writing, in that Fuchs describes essential failings of capitalism while he denies authority to all ideological positions, including anticapitalism. On the one hand, his most effective means of deprecating the profit motive in American society is to dissolve the boundary between legitimate commercial enterprise and the crime world. The activities of gangsters in his fiction are an extension of ordinary business, and his businessmen are, often consciously, incipient criminals in their exploitiveness. On the other hand, while conveying this social view, Fuchs uses various means to suggest as well that any position of certainty, including his own attack on capitalism, is but a limited perspective. His major device toward that end is to avoid the use of heroes and otherwise to mock the education novel, which depends on an assumed system of values. His undercutting of cultural truths spares one value alone, a pervasive theme of his—the need for fellow feeling.

The fact that critics have widely differed about Fuchs's tone toward his characters suggests that his novels are not simple. Howe found at one time an absence and later a presence of authorial sympathy in the fiction.[36] While Madden observes that "Fuchs' eye is compassionate, his laughter gentle,"[37] Halper writes that "Fuchs hates all his characters. When he writes with pity, it is a merciless, steely, stiletto kind of pity."[38] Like Madden, Harold Beaver finds no such hatred in Fuchs, but "a peculiar blend of irony with good humor."[39] In a favorable *New York Times* review of the three novels in 1961, Robert Gorham Davis is uncertain "where [Fuchs] stands in relation to his material."[40] Farrell, commenting on *Low Company,* writes that "sympathy is a dominant note in Fuchs' writing. . . . No matter how repulsive his characters may be . . . he portrays them with sympathy."[41] This complicatedness in unpleasant and even gruesome characters, a hallmark of masterful characterization, has led one commentator to the curious complaint about Fuchs's writing that "the grotesquerie of so many of [the] characters intrudes on his perception of them."[42]

Though it is not the primary objective of this study, I hope to demonstrate that Fuchs's ambiguities derive from the sort of bewilderment that Hawthorne described in *The House of the Seven Gables* as the measure of a man's wisdom. As inconsolable through doctrine as Ecclesiastes, Fuchs, too, surveys the widespread folly and inequity under the (American) sun. He produces no solution, only a picture well wrought, though, like Anderson, West, Faulkner, Crane, and other American writers who fit this description, he is more than a photographer. Fuchs is one of those writers who, in the words of F. R. Leavis, "[finding] no such approach to tradition and orthodoxy [as that of T. S. Eliot] possible, can only cultivate the sense of health we have."[43] Struck by America's failure to change human nature, Fuchs fashions his ambivalences into an appropriate creative response.

These ambivalences will be a unifying element in the following discussion of the Brooklyn novels. The work is divided into two parts. Chapters 2 and 3 will deal with the dynamics between Fuchs's social criticism, conveyed largely through use of underworld figures, and his modernist devices to import philosophical questioning into the novels. Following that analysis will be three chapters devoted to a close reading of each of the novels, with focus on the correspondence between Fuchs's epistemological and artistic skepticism.

2
The Gangster as Theme

Fuchs's brand of realism inheres in the relationship between his social criticism and his artistic vision. He comments socially in portraying a continuum between the businessman and the criminal, yet he suggests the elusiveness of any authoritative position. In this chapter I will discuss the first of these elements, providing some context for Fuchs's use of the gangster figure.

The gangster has become as much part of American mythology as the cowboy, and Fuchs gives gangsters a prominent part in each of the novels.[1] Despite the differences in the three narrative structures, all three novels have in common a social vision largely communicated through the use of underworld figures. Fuchs develops as his central metaphor the evolution of the crime industry in America as it corresponds to the history of all commercial enterprise. Though the three novels deal with entirely separate sets of characters, they reflect an advance in organization and influence from the autonomous lawbreaker, Uncle Papravel in *Summer in Williamsburg,* who shrewdly acquires a transit monopoly, to the impersonal underworld force in *Low Company* that is too vast to identify or comprehend. In all three novels Fuchs obscures the distinction between legitimate business and the business of crime. This continuum between criminals and businessmen makes the problem of capitalism the backdrop for the dramas of individual lives. The problem, as Fuchs illustrates it, is that, with capital as the greatest good, ruthlessness becomes the greatest means. According to the profit-motivated society he portrays, not only is crime an industry, industry is a crime in its destruction of human values. A more organized system destroys more efficiently.

"Where but in America could a man do so well by himself?" Uncle Papravel asks Rubin, his partner in violence and extortion (100), whom he is about to betray. Papravel's business is modest, his henchmen including the killer Gilhooley and "one Negro, two Jews, and three Italians." These are sufficient to terrorize the rival bus-company owner, Morand, by beatings and vandalism, so that he will yield his lucrative route to the Catskills. Papravel's ethic establishes the confusion of legitimate and illegitimate enterprise that will be essential in the three novels. He tells his nephew Harry:

> What I know only is, a man's got to make money. Everybody who makes money hurts people. Sometimes you can't see the people you are hurting, but you can be sure all the time there is always somebody who gets squeezed if he is not ruined. That's the kind of a world it is, and who am I to change it? Only, in my business you can see the people you hurt and that's what makes you hate it. . . . No matter what business you'll be in, remember there will always be people who live in rotten houses, who will have no money for a good time and who will die ten years earlier on account of you. (P. 253)

Papravel's homily is supported throughout *Summer in Williamsburg.* Old Miller's greed causes him to be swindled by confidence men selling fake jewels. The old cynic makes his living by selling prayers at the cemetery. Philip acknowledges in a letter to his wealthy friend Charles Nagleman that money is "a dirty business in itself" (117). Mrs. Van Curen, owner of the boardinghouse in Havers Falls, is so dazzled by the extra three dollars for each new hoodlum she shelters that she swears to the virtues of Papravel, her benefactor, "even though he was a Jew" (129). This benefactor suffers distress when his henchman Gilhooley shoots a policeman, not on account of scruples but because as a businessman he would now be "associated with the signs of common thuggery and gangsterism" (238). Set off against Papravel's enterprising energy is the passivity of Max Hayman, who appears as a specter to his son Harry, and who disdains the profit motive to his own disadvantage, even in legitimate dealings.

The second novel uses Blenholt's symbolic position as Commissioner of Sewers to extend the picture of crookedness to politics, a connection familiar to newspaper readers in the thirties. The late celebrated Commissioner, whom the reader meets only through reminiscences of him, shares with the more modestly enterprising Papravel a benevolence that endears him to his underlings. He bore all responsibility and worry for his men, hovering over them "like an army of angels."[2] In the novel's central scene at the funeral, prolix testimonials to Blenholt's philanthropy are brought to a halt by someone in the audience bold and angered enough to denounce Blenholt's racketeering practices.

> "All his outings and charities, who paid for it? Me! Me and every other little store-keeper and push-cart peddler on the block, every

week we paid for it and for plenty more! Good money we made with
sweat and blood we had to give out of our own pockets. Give, he said
and the bums with the pistols in their hands said give, and we gave
like it was a hold-up, we gave! We gave until we got pushed out of
business altogether. Like me!" (P. 164)

Dismissed as a Communist and a lunatic, the man is quieted so
that the program may proceed with a speaker representing the
respectable Ladies' Aid Auxiliary. In *Summer in Williamsburg*
Papravel appears benevolent in the eyes of Mrs. Van Curen; in
Homage to Blenholt the corrupt commissioner is honored as benevolent by respectable society at large. And in the second novel
Max Balkan, unlike Philip Hayman, subscribes unequivocally to
the belief in wealth. Balkan has no qualms over the tactics by which
his idol has achieved his eminence, because power is the magic that
keeps eluding him, the power to achieve wealth and the power that
wealth brings.

In *Low Company* a thug called "the sniffler" describes the syndicate as "a combination now. . . . on a large scale, same as a chain-
store system" (78).[3] It has an orderly "bail and lawyer fund"
supported by tribute from prostitutes and madams (87), and it is so
widespread that "they don't want no independents in the business.
They're taking over" (148). The sniffler tells a fellow henchman, "I
got no use personally for guns and shooting. Rough stuff. It's out of
date, behind the times. I like organization and smart handling.
Businesslike, see? What the hell, if you can't operate like any
ordinary business, you never last long" (209).

The syndicate makes purging New York of all independent criminals (255) part of its pervasive and intricate business. The hoodlums, careworn by their responsibilities—"the whole burden rested
on him alone" (300)—follow the commands of a local boss with
absolute murderous intent who is sad-eyed, "looking weary and
worried." "This business is not a picnic exactly," he complains
(237). While Fuchs represents the crime world as evil and deadly, he
keeps underscoring its continuity with ordinary commerce. The
syndicate boss, for example, who defines business as taking care of
worries by any means, is introduced immediately following the
savage beating of Karty by his brothers-in-law, legitimate businessmen who own a garage and are trying by any means to recover
their stolen capital.

Spitzbergen and Shubunka, who are in league to sell sexual
pleasure, are able by that means to give people employment and
earn prestige as "men of money" (270–71). Ann, Spitzbergen's well-

dressed wife, is sympathetic when she learns about her husband's illegal activities: "A righteous man had no place in business" is her ironic comment on the evening of Spitzbergen's death. The values that Fuchs exposes are most tellingly conveyed in Ann's assessment of her husband's profiting from prostitution: "She could not hold him to practices that could lead only to losses" (157–58). The pervasiveness of Papravel's ethic through the other two Brooklyn novels is demonstrated by a remark from Herbert Lurie, the most fairminded and alert of *Low Company*'s characters. As owner of a shop, Lurie regards himself as a participant in a culpable system. After Shubunka confesses his monstrous business as a whoremonger, Lurie replies with Papravel's point: "I'm not a hypocrite," he says. "Business is business. It's the same goddamned thing in my line, only a little less lousy" (181).

As the title of Fuchs's first published article, "Where Al Capone Grew Up," suggests, he was preoccupied from the start of his writing career with the gangster as a person, and he had several resources to help shape his underworld images. His oldest brother, Abraham Rupert, who abandoned his first name when he was a high-school football star, became an auto mechanic with gangster contacts. Rupert brought home stories about "shtarkes," thugs who extorted and even killed for a living, stories that made their impact on the future novelist.[4] Fuchs's other main resources were the contemporary criminal world in New York, especially Brooklyn, which was the subject of prodigious journalistic attention, and the representation of gangsters in American movies of the early thirties.

Prohibition under the Volstead Act, 1919–33, not only fostered the careers of smalltime racketeers who became as famous in their way as Jesse James; it also engaged great numbers of normally lawabiding citizens in bootlegging and illegal drinking, thereby muddying definitions of illicit and respectable conduct. The most brilliant and influential gangland personality in the twenties was Arnold Rothstein, on whom Fitzgerald partly based his Meyer Wolfsheim in *The Great Gatsby*. Before Rothstein's unsolved murder in 1928, he was head of a crime syndicate called by its members The Combination, which brought smalltime gambling, prostitution, money-lending, extortion, and professional violence into the era of organization. Son of a reputable clothing manufacturer, Rothstein used his charm and polish to mingle with high society, glamorizing his gambling activities and—like Philip Hayman's Uncle Papravel, Commissioner of Sewers Blenholt, and Louis Spitzbergen—blurring the line between American enterprise and felony. As a theatrical "angel" and legitimate real-estate broker at the same time as he was a rumrunner and narcotics tycoon, Rothstein eluded prosecution but not attention. Newspapers carried full-page spreads about his adventures and his celebrated coolness.

Rothstein, whom Damon Runyon called "The Brain," moved comfortably between the underworld and respectable society, maintaining an office with a professional staff in the downtown business district. Eventually, by "consolidating various aspects of the underworld, from gang life on its most elementary level to sophisticated and complicated business deals, [Rothstein was] largely responsible for putting crime 'on a corporate basis.' "[5] His heirs, Murder, Inc., although without his Manhattan polish, adopted his businesslike procedures. Murder is also part of the business operation of the organization that crushes Shubunka in *Low Company*. He is taking profits that they can make theirs simply by ridding Neptune of him, and their superior organization prevails over his small enterprise. This corporate business interest is served by those in its lower ranks whose job it is to follow assignments, without having to understand the total system.

Underworld activities were not remote journalistic curiosities to inhabitants of the Coney Island area, including Fuchs before and during the time he was writing his novels. In 1937, the year that Vanguard published *Low Company*, Louis "Lepke" Buchalter had been hiding out for two years from Special State Prosecutor Thomas Dewey at a Coney Island recreational facility, the Oriental Danceland. While in hiding, Lepke was reported in the newspapers to have met regularly with Albert Anastasia and other members of the Combination to "contract" the murders of former business associates who might inform on him.[6]

Fuchs writes of his own acquaintance with the gangsters in those days:

> They were all around, hard to miss, in the candystores, on the street. . . . Mad Dog Vincent Coll was shot down in the phone booth in Hell's Kitchen around the corner from P. S. 11 where I was teaching. My brother Rupert, in the battery & ignition business, worked on the rum runners' boats operating out of Sheepshead Bay (next door to Brighton Beach. . . .) Later, he worked on Owney Madden's laundry trucks, when Madden controlled that business. (All this perfectly legitimate work. They offered Rupert large sums to go out with the boats; he demurred.) His good friend was an ex-gangster and I'd see something of him. When I taught school, I used to stop by at my brother's place on Bedford Avenue on my way to Pratt Library (where

W. Whitman did some writing). The thugs lounging about my brother's place used to tip their hats to me, out of respect for my profession.[7]

Fuchs was well acquainted with another image of the gangster, the screen portrayal. Though the official viewpoint of both journalism and cinema was that even glamorous enemies of society deserve retribution, the actual filmic attitude was more ambivalent. The engaging qualities of popular actors playing the antisocial protagonists contributed to that moral complexity. Yet while in real life the retribution did not always happen, in Hollywood's versions it was required, by the Hays Production Code if not by dramatic formula. The filmmaker emphasized the personality of the underworld figure and how he—and sometimes she—came to that career, rather than the real effects of crime, but that protagonist, no matter how appealing, was obliged to meet a harsh and usually violent end. The fact that he or she was so appealing put the audience in an ambiguous emotional position.

Fuchs was eighteen when talking was added to the screen image in 1927, and within three years the gangster movie capitalized on the dimension of sound as well as inventive camera techniques to produce more lifelike treatment than had been feasible before. The first four years of the thirties, the period during which Fuchs composed his first novel, were a meteoric period of vigor for the genre of the gangster film. In 1931 alone there were fifty gangster films.[8] But as Federal programs brought hope to the country, attention in the film stories turned toward the supporting (though just as violent) members of society rather than the renegades, and forces of protest organized successfully against the glorifying of criminal life. With a few important exceptions the genre was finished by 1934, its harsh attitude eventually replaced by one more optimistic; audiences became receptive to the notion typified by the films of director Frank Capra, that all people, if given an opportunity, are basically decent and generous. By the late thirties, both the hard realism and the defiant tone of gangster films were anomalies. Ironically, Fuchs, who was attuned to the skepticism of the genre, went to Hollywood to write films, many of them dealing with gangsters, in this new atmosphere.

The success of the gangster film genre depended largely on the confrontation and tension between two ideas. One of these is the Horatio Alger myth fundamental to America's immigrant culture, inherent in the nation's youth, vastness, and natural resources—the formula in which eventual triumph rewards one who is determined, diligent, and adept at a particular set of rules. The opposing idea is the public ethic, whereby a wrongdoer's actions must doom him or her. On the one hand the movie gangster is a Boy Who Makes Good. He typically comes from poor immigrant parents and has been unfairly dealt with. He is almost always played by an actor who is short in stature (Cagney, Robinson, Raft, Muni), as if to emphasize his small chances in the tough city, as opposed to the tall Western hero, who has some advantages in facing similarly discouraging odds. From these humble beginnings the gangster acquires power and wealth, friends, fine clothing, an automobile, and occasionally a blonde. He has found success in America. On the other hand, he thrives on violence, gets so deep into intrigue that he loses a measure of control, and adds to his criminality the overextension of his ego. What he wants, the protagonist of *Little Caesar* says, is "more." Most satisfying to the audience and yet the most perilous of his qualities is his opposition to the forces of authority in America.

This collision of values, which both responds to and fosters the ambivalence gripping its spectators, is epitomized in the 1930 film *Little Caesar,* based on W. R. Burnett's 1929 novel of the same title and starring Edward G. Robinson. Its oxymoronic title adds to the film's appropriateness as the classic representative of the gangster film and exemplifies the complicated attitude toward criminals that prevailed when Fuchs was writing. Reversing a decline in movie attendance, *Little Caesar* began the four-year apogee of a genre which showed the recognizable grimness of poverty and the striving to escape it. The audience could forget for a time that the criminal's fate had been decided by his or her first antisocial deed, either before or at the beginning of the picture. For a time they could admire the memorable personality they would ultimately have to reject as their scapegoat. Stuart Kaminsky writes about the genre, "Society worships ruthless ambition, but insists that we love our neighbor. . . . We root for the gangster—and are guiltily gratified when he is gunned down."[9]

In his essay about the gangster film, "The Gangster as Tragic Hero," Robert Warshow makes the point that, as an inhabitant of the modern city, and even its personification, the gangster is required to succeed in order to emerge from the crowd. His only possibility being failure, "the final meaning of the city is anonymity and death." Warshow concludes: "In the deeper layers of the modern consciousness, *all* means are unlawful, every attempt to succeed is an act of aggression. . . . Our intolerable dilemma [is] that failure is a kind of death and success is evil and dangerous," even impossible.[10] Like Nietzsche's sacrifice of the tragic figure in *The Birth of Tragedy*, the gangster's death in the film momentarily resolves that dilemma.

Fuchs fills his novels with direct references to the impact of movies on his characters, including the substance of their reveries and their education in how to kiss, how to walk, and how to light a cigar. His use of the gangster figure in particular, however, shows an ambivalence about the criminal in America very like that reflected in the genre that thrived from 1930 to 1934, with a corresponding implicit social comment. The gangster, dislocated, solitary, ultimately smashed by the system that calls out its lures to him, is an apt emblem for the Depression. In Kaminsky's words, "The gangster films of the 1930s . . . were generally semi-conscious attempts to deal with the Depression and the public's shaken confidence in American economics, politics, and myths of the self-made man."[11] Film historian Arthur Knight observes:

> The pictures of the early thirties reflected the national disaster. The drawing-room comedies, the sophisticated plays, even the "canned" musicals—the staples of the first years of sound—had begun to pall. As banks failed and lifelong savings were wiped out, as unemployment spread . . . , audiences sought a more recognizable image of their own problems on the screen. . . . What the public obviously wanted was a hard-hitting, naturalistic form of drama that took its themes from the headlines of the day.[12]

With women as well as men showing by their lives on screen that living outside the law was the only means of escape from despair, what was bound to result was what Kaminsky calls "the ambivalence of the genre, which both admires and rejects the gangster."[13] Fuchs's outlaw figures are portrayed with a similar complexity, and no other serious writer of the thirties made them so central and yet so unromanticized.

Though Fuchs's Brooklyn novels were composed within less than five years, his uses of the gangster in the three works are diverse in both how they function in the plot and how they express a worldview. *Summer in Williamsburg* depicts the choice between honesty and wealth during an era which intensified this struggle. Like many of the young men in Fuchs's short stories, Philip cannot aspire to marry the young woman he would like. As a creature of the city Philip must find a way to make his living, and no way aside from his uncle's offers itself. But his father's moral presence is sufficient to neutralize Papravel's temptation, and at the end of the novel it is not certain what compromise his brother Harry has carved for himself or how Philip will proceed. The sources of the uncle's jubilation in the final scene do not include victory in the lives of his nephews.

In *Summer in Williamsburg* the issue of moral choice looms, with Mr. Hayman's virtue and powerlessness on the one side, and Uncle Papravel's corruption and success on the other. As in the other novels, Fuchs mutes the problem of unemployment and instead poses the issue of the quality of jobs available to his young men. Harry, who associates Williamsburg with the smell of vinegar, dreads being one of the high-school graduates who "troop home from the subway exits in a line, with the dried perspiration and irritating clothes of workers, swinging their folded newspapers at their sides as a symbol" (257). He wants not just to earn a living but to live with joy and luxury, as people do in the movies.

Papravel as the gangster figure in this novel functions as a tempter to corruption who remains a human being, his humanity making the alternative he offers more attractive. Fuchs calls attention to the personalities of Papravel and his men, to Papravel's good will toward his sister and her family, to his sister's fondness for him, and to his lack of bitterness at the repudiation by all three Hayman men. Though what he does to his rival, Morand, is monstrous, Papravel is somehow no monster, and not merely because Morand returns the violence. Papravel and his henchmen are appealing to Philip.

At Havers Falls, after Philip refrains from sending his wealthy friend Charles Nagleman a letter because he fears it is pretentiously worded, he adapts his language to the company of the thugs, "playing five-cent stud poker, talking, smoking and drinking wine, like respectable business men after work. Call them what you want, Philip said, they are grown-up" (119). Harry's remarks about his bookish brother call attention to the contrast between this group's manliness and Philip's studies of Chaucer and Elizabethan drama, a contrast strengthened by the academic diction in his letter to Charles that had made Philip uneasy. Hearing the men laughing and exchanging stories, "Philip forgot they were racketeers, hold-up men, and gangsters. He even liked them. . . . They, too, are children of God, he said, and they make money in their own fashion" (120–21). As he reflects that night on the impotence of abstract philosophy, Philip comes closer than at any other point to joining his uncle's gang; only "the picture of his father, pained and broken, stopped him" (121).

The problem Philip and Harry face is never solved. Philip waits to see what will become of himself. Harry's future, too, is uncertain because he seems persuaded by his uncle's view of legitimate earnings: "The way he's got it figured out, if I open a haberdashery store in Grand Street three women and four kids will live stunted lives" (279). No option that corresponds to Mr. Hayman's scruples is available, yet his influence weighs against Papravel's persuasiveness and keeps his sons in a perpetual inner debate.

Homage to Blenholt also portrays a gangster chief and his henchmen, but in this case the gangster, Blenholt, has died before the novel begins, and the protagonists have never met him. That unfamiliarity changes the quality of his influence on the character who emulates him, Max Balkan. Though the reader never meets Blenholt, his portrait gradually comes into shape to justify Max's reverence, because Blenholt did wield the power that Max longs for, yet at the same time to mock that reverence because Blenholt's power is so inaccessible for Max.

Like Papravel, Blenholt was avuncular. His grieving "cutthroats" recall not only the glamor he had brought to their lives, but also their freedom from responsibility in following his orders. But Blenholt, the Commissioner of Sewers and therefore the consummate underground ruler, possessed greater and broader power than Papravel. The grandeur of his funeral supports Max's view of Blenholt as the modern Tamburlaine, Xerxes, or Caesar. Interdenominational in his influence, the late Commissioner spoke Yiddish at synagogues and Italian at Catholic weddings, though he was perhaps a Turk.

Blenholt, like Papravel, embodies an alternative to the powerlessness of the young protagonist's father, but not an alternative that is available to the young man, Max Balkan. Though Label Balkan is more ridiculous in his failure and therefore less attractive an example than Philip Hayman's father, in the second novel the choice is not posed between Blenholt's moral deficiency and any qualities that Max's father possesses. The powerlessness of both Balkans is framed not in a moral but in a pragmatic conflict, in which the counterbalance to absence of power is not the value of integrity but the inaccessibility of Blenholt's lifestyle and wealth. What most defines the absurdity of Max Balkan's aspirations is the remoteness of success.

Max romanticizes Blenholt as a modern Tamburlaine. The real glimpses of Blenholt, a diabetic who has succumbed to sweets, and of his pathetically leaderless thugs are at Max's expense. A fundamental distinction between the first two novels is that Max's choices are not real because his information is not real, and so the reader becomes disengaged from him as an amused spectator. From the outset, Max's determination to pay homage to this stranger makes him a figure of humor. The role of the gangster in *Homage to*

Blenholt is not, then, to pose any real alternative, as in *Summer in Williamsburg,* but to underscore Max's futile and naive means of dealing with his cramped life options. While the ugliness of the prospects facing Max and his friends is much the same as what confronts the Hayman brothers, Fuchs wrings some mirth out of misery by making his young men clumsy and impractical. He moves his focus from moral rubrics to the ineptitude that is as much a barrier to success as economic conditions. The ambiguity of the novel results from Fuchs's subverting the reader's inclination to become engaged with a protagonist's striving against odds to achieve dreams of glory and triumph over humiliation.

In *Low Company* Fuchs uses the gangster motif more integrally and more darkly in the novel's structure. The character who at first appears to correspond to Papravel and Blenholt is Shubunka, whose business is running brothels and who enjoys material success and therefore a kind of esteem. His is a grudging and painful esteem, however, circumscribed by an immense ugliness that repels people. In the course of the novel's two days, Shubunka is crushed by a far more powerful underworld force, so that he becomes, unlike Papravel and Blenholt (who was victim only of himself), abused by others. The victim function is rearranged to include even the story's moral monster. This rearrangement is consistent with the novel's motif of circularity.

What makes the gangster's force more menacing in *Low Company* than in the other novels is its anonymity and ubiquity. The crime world that has decided to reach into Neptune Beach is as mysterious and inexorable as Joseph K.'s oppressors. There is no eluding its agents as they carry out their assigned tasks and report to superiors. Though their conversations show them to be the same small and ordinary men as in the other novels, they serve an organization far more terrifying than Papravel's or Blenholt's.

The efficient and omnipresent invading organization dwarfs Shubunka's criminality. Absurd as his histrionics may be, he is humanly representative in his ironic pleading on moral grounds, "It's not right!" His business of illicit pleasures appears less destructive than their cool slaughtering, more like an extension of the short-lived sweets sold at Ann's soda shop. The effect of Shubunka's helplessness in relation to such a force is to diffuse moral categories among the primary characters.

Whereas the first novel delineates choices and the second novel mocks them, the third by and large disregards them. Fuchs operates in *Low Company* at the intersection of realism and determinism, with all his characters but one subject to their circumstances and their compulsions. Herbert Lurie alone, through his response to Shubunka, comes to terms with the humanity at Neptune Beach; that experience is made possible only by Shubunka's persistence in intruding his humanity into another character's world. Lurie hears the gangster and is affected.

The role of the gangster figure, then, serves the indeterminacies central to each of the novels. In *Summer in Williamsburg* Uncle Papravel's ruthlessness is the greatest evil the reader encounters, yet Fuchs does not simply reject his mode of living. In *Homage to Blenholt* the comic treatment of Max's hero-worship separates the reader from the one character most likely to invite sympathy. In *Low Company* understandable commercial motives like those behind the dealings of Papravel, Blenholt, and Shubunka have gone out of control. With those in command ultimately unknowable, the magnitude of the underworld system bespeaks a new era, in which the methodical destruction of a man like a cockroach is a business decision. The process of dehumanization, as Fuchs depicts it, results from the ethic of all business—in its continuum from legitimate to criminal enterprise—which is to make judgments on the basis of profit.

3
Style and Technique: Doubting Perspectives

Because of the accuracy of his phonography, especially though not exclusively of the Yiddish idiom, Fuchs has been called chiefly an observer.[1] Indeed, his strength in dialogue has associated him with the *tranche de vie* naturalists. But Fuchs intended to avoid the flatness of Stendhal's ideal "court record." Both through the character Philip Hayman and in his own published remarks about writing fiction, Fuchs regards as a necessary evil the artist's task of imposing artifice, a "concocted ordering," on the details of honest observation. Fuchs's ordering balances attention to social ills against attention to individual foibles to reflect the problematics of responsibility. His attitude toward his characters is elusive in that, instead of arousing sympathies to support a social position, he assembles his portraits so as to mitigate aroused sympathies; in this way Fuchs questions moral certainty. His ambiguities support the notion of comprehensiveness—inclusiveness—as the means to comprehension. Instead of a "concocted ordering" that locates credibility within a simplifyingly salient protagonist, Fuchs's notion of inclusiveness requires an ordering that distributes credibility.

Fuchs's objectivity is achieved, then, not by the absence of sympathies but by the play of competing sympathies. Fuchs invites the reader to enter each character's consciousness and predicament. The effect of having all of the characters in turn make their claim on the reader's understanding is to limit the claim of any one character. This equivocation of sympathies is consistent with Fuchs's taking up and then renouncing or subverting various notions. For example, he offers and dismisses scientific determinism in *Summer in Williamsburg,* undermines the polarities of sentimentality and satire in *Homage to Blenholt,* and hedges on utter pessimism in *Low Company.*

Fuchs's mutually disrupting interpretations have an effect similar to the density produced through the use of an unreliable narrator. But he goes a step beyond this device by which an authoritative voice implies what is unreliable. Philip Hayman's resemblance to a portrait of the artist notwithstanding, in all three novels Fuchs variously subverts patterns of association between the reader and major characters. The three major techniques that I will discuss as Fuchs's means to test notions about absolute perception are the multiple protagonist, the telegraphically jarring shift in perspective, and the symbolic use of doors and mirrors to focus on the mystery of perspective.

Tension exists in the novels not only between the consciousness of protagonists and the dynamics of their society, but also in the fragmenting of the protagonist role. This distributed focus is the basis for Fuchs's other devices. It will be useful to distinguish between two types of plural protagonists, although Fuchs uses both. For purposes of this discussion the term "collective protagonist" means the group as a whole functioning as the main character, as Steinbeck's Joad family functions, for example. The term "multiple protagonist" means the division of the protagonist function among several main individual characters, as in *Ulysses* and *The Sound and the Fury*.

The line between collective and multiple protagonist is not always distinct, even in *The Grapes of Wrath*. While the Joad family—expanded to include the preacher Casy—is the collective protagonist, there is sufficient individuation of some of the characters for them to be regarded as multiple protagonists. Fuchs's writing, too, falls into some middle area, and both Steinbeck and Fuchs use the technique of multiple protagonists so as to retain the reader's concentration on the group.

A more important distinction between the two writers, however, has to do with ideology. George Becker, in a study of European realism, observes two related uses of the group protagonist. "It provides a gamut of personalities and situations that, to the extent that they are subject to the same causal influences, give the illusion of an adequate induction." And "by a spread of emphasis, such an approach reduces the importance of the single protagonist, who by definition is too salient a figure for a realistic work."[2] Becker's explanation contains a paradox, in his reference to both an adequate induction and the pluralistic requirement of realism. This is the paradox that Fuchs tries to deal with: the coexistence of a distribution of credibility and the unifying credibility invoked by the collective picture. Put more simply, Steinbeck's celebration of the spirit of community is his adequate induction, but Fuchs doubts not only the possibilities of that spirit but also the salience of the induction.

The succession of contending perspectives becomes a progressively more organic device in the three Brooklyn novels. Both *Summer in Williamsburg* and *Homage to Blenholt* contain a young man who appears to signal the traditional education novel. But in the first novel Fuchs breaks from that convention by dividing his focus in two ways: between the sensitive and ambivalent young man, a type of Jude or Stephen Dedalus, and the tenement as a struggling (collective) social entity, and also, within the collective view, between the young man and two contemporaries, his brother and his best friend, who are in crisis as well.

In *Homage to Blenholt* Fuchs turns the education-novel formula inside out. The idealistic Max Balkan and his two young eccentric friends, as well as Max's father Label, possess appealing qualities and are abused by the world. But not only does Fuchs detach the reader from them by making them a group of comic grotesques, he also uses their perspectives on one another as a further means to limit their salience.

In the third novel Fuchs separates suffering from goodness. By mitigating both the wickedness and virtue of his characters as they alternately inflict and suffer abuse, he deprives the reader of a hero by any definition. The reader's emotional involvement must come from some source other than attachment to one character, or even to the group ideologically defined. Increasingly in the three novels Fuchs choreographs his characters in the manner of Sherwood Anderson in *Winesburg, Ohio,* in that, while the group's experiences are the major interest beyond those of any single character, the group never takes on ideological meaning.

In *Summer in Williamsburg* the reader is invited to be most fully engaged in the consciousness of Philip, whose view of things is so credited that some critics mistake him for the narrator.[3] Philip, though, is often entirely removed from the action. He is absent during the episodes dealing with Sam Linck and his women, Tessie and her bridegroom, the bus monopoly war, and Cohen as he jumps off the bridge. During the time that Philip is away from Williamsburg at Havers Falls, from Chapter 7 to the beginning of Chapter 10, the narrative turns to the vicissitudes of other characters. This new focus is aside from the novel's panorama from childhood to old age in the tenement and neighborhood; it is particularly directed to Philip's brother Harry and Philip's closest friend Cohen. Harry and Cohen assume part of the burden of collecting, sorting, and interpreting information—the function which from the outset has characterized Philip. All three qualify as "reflecting consciousnesses."

That the nineteen characters of *Summer* are involved in an intricate design becomes most evident during Philip's absence from Williamsburg, when the narrative focus is widened. The omniscient narrator, summarizing, weaves together four separate events: 1) Old Man Miller's betrayal and stroke, 2) Sam Linck's beating by Marge's henchmen, 3) Mrs. Sussman's departure with her children to seek a new life in Montana, and 4) Tessie's wedding (115). Vital scenes occur while Philip is away during Chapter 8 feeling homesick for Williamsburg: Tessie's loveless marriage, his friend Cohen's jump from a bridge, little Davey's adventure with a horse, and Old Miller's death.

Philip has been advised by Miller to "collect" in order to know about life, but while he is out of the narrative picture either the narrator collects or another character does. By this device there is no lapse in the palpable details of everyday Williamsburg. In effect, the reader becomes the collector.

Harry and Cohen serve some functions that are consistent with the use of Philip as a single protagonist. The two are diverse and balancing foils to Philip in their contrasting ways of life; the extravagant romanticism displaced onto Cohen, for example, allows him to bear the taint of the *bildungsroman* hero, offsetting Philip's practicality, somewhat as with Tom Sawyer and Huck Finn, and Harry's accommodation to crime emphasizes Philip's moral sensitivity. But aside from showing that Philip's crisis is not unique, these characters, particularly Harry, also take on more than an ordinary amount of the central figure's inner debate.

Philip's friend Cohen is a hysteric; his every impulse is exaggerated, he is consumed with thoughts of the soul and Russian novels, and one of his favorite subjects is suicide. His anguished search for self often appears to be a cartoon variation of Philip's struggle. Cohen's efforts at significant attachment, chiefly his flirtation with the Communist party, contain no doubt the sharpest satire in the novel. Yet in scenes with Cohen alone, his "collecting" is fully as observant as Philip's, and though he is a "schlemiel," his imagination and his desperation elicit sympathy.

> Cohen climbed down from the pedestrian walks to the paths for the automobiles. He scaled the railing here. Below was the East River, somber, undulatingly fearsome. The red and green lights of the tugs and barges looked up at him. What are you doing? they blinked, like children in their wonder. What's the matter with you? (P. 155)

With no family to give emotional support like Philip's, he is another of Philip's confused and purposeless generation whose creativity is strangled by the absence of opportunity.

Harry, too, is of Philip's generation, faced with the same choice between comfort and integrity. Though Harry finds "something ugly about physical violence" (20), he belongs to his uncle's gang of thugs. Harry, the character who lets the reader know that Philip is a college student, appears literate himself. He writes well and refers to Chaucer and Elizabethan drama, and Fuchs occasionally abandons Philip's *agon* for Harry's. A number of passages dealing with Harry describe the crisis of choice that would conventionally belong to the education novel's central figure.

After Papravel's homily on ethics and money, the writing focuses on Harry as the one who collects, wonders, suffers, experiences epiphanies, evaluates, decides, and philosophizes (258). The description of Harry's visit home sounds very like a turning point for a protagonist.

> He was dismayed with the hopelessness that he saw in his father's droop. . . . [H]e seemed older and drier and thinner. . . . All at once a rush of sorrow swept Harry, then sorrow and pain. He seemed to understand his father and his meaning with sudden clarity and sharpness. In a wave of tenderness he wanted to put his arms around his father, tell him he was right, hug him, and shout out cheerful sounds. At the moment he loved his father more than he had ever loved anything in his life. (P. 255)

But after a night of tears accompanying a range of impressions of his father and his own situation, Harry awakes to the ugliness of Williamsburg. Hearing a woman's shrill scream, he asks a boy in the hallway what the matter is:

> "Nothing, nothing," he said. It was an old story to him and the accident itself was minor. "Mrs. Glickner put her kid into the bath-tub in cold water on account of its being hot. The kid got up and turned the hot water on. He burned himself."

Harry returns to his flat certain that he cannot remain at home. "The odor of lox, frying in onions, filled his nostrils" (259). By giving so much weight to Harry's troubles Fuchs diminishes Philip's centrality.

Many of the characters' tribulations in *Homage to Blenholt* are brought on by themselves. With Fuchs's harsh comic treatment, the shifts from scene to scene bring relief as they interlace the crises of

Max Balkan with those of other characters, chiefly his two friends, Munves and Coblenz, and the boy Heshey. Fuchs still has a primary protagonist, as he does not in the third novel, but the fortunes of the other three characters in the same tenement receive sufficient attention to prevent the story from being only his. These fortunes are resolved interdependently when Coblenz's gift of his gambling winnings enables Max and Munves to settle their fate in the delicatessen business, with Munves marrying Max's sister.

In *Low Company,* Fuchs's elaborate cyclical design is entirely inseparable from theme. In this work more than in the others he blends the collective and the multiple protagonist. While achieving his strongest character delineations, particularly in the brothel-keeper Shubunka, Fuchs shifts attention from one individual to the next and back again as they all bewail their injuries while injuring one another. The disturbing result is a protagonist fashioned out of both a suffering and a persecuting community. This comprehensive approach to the group is in distinct contrast with the use of an ideological collective protagonist, whose enemy is an outside force.

These uses of the plural protagonist in Fuchs's novels have their antecedents in Europe and America. The fiction writer in Europe who devoted almost the whole of his work to the study of group as hero and whose work Fuchs read and discussed was Jules Romains (1885–1972).[4] Romains's theory, called "l'unanisme," gave a more psychological emphasis to the interest of writers including Zola and Balzac in fully portraying society with a great number of characters. The theory holds that a group functioning together fuses into a new individuality. Though appearing to diverge extremely from Proust's and Gide's preoccupation with the individual, the theory of unanism responds as well to the problem of spiritual chaos.[5] The dread of being solitary is a probable source of both the expression of private metaphysical *angst* and the effort to lose oneself in action among a group, the loss being, of course, a form of gain or release.

More like Whitman than Zola, Romains saw the community as continuous with a universal collectivity which is fully conscious of its distinct and divine being. Most twentieth-century writers who have treated the group as possessing a persona have represented its behavior as alarming, instead of as more evolved than that of its particular members, as can be seen especially in the violent conclusions of Friedrich Dürrenmatt's *The Visit of the Old Lady* and Nathanael West's *The Day of the Locust*.

While Fuchs participates in this modern difference from Romains, like Romains he depicts the claims that the group makes on the individual. For example. Philip Hayman's search for a way to live his life takes him to the mountains. He finds the healthful serenity there alienating and cannot wait to return to the mordancy of Williamsburg, where he experiences at least some fellow feeling. A character in Romains's *La Vie Unanime* tries to flee from society and modern city life to nature's refuge, but his initial feeling of triumph is short-lived. Romains shows, according to critic J. B. Norrish, that a person "cannot endure solitude without suffering, without a sensation of drowning, and so the escapist, terrified by nature, turns back to 'les unanimes,' yearning for 'un peu de fluide humain'. . . . He prefers to be drowned by society, which has more compensation to offer."[6] Nathanael West depicts a similar response in the idyll of Miss Lonelyhearts and Betty, when the sound of birds and crickets in the country is "a horrible racket" in his ears; all he sees in the shaded wood is death, "rotten leaves, gray and white fungi, and over everything a funereal hush."[7]

The claims of community are evident as well in *Homage* and *Low Company*. It never occurs to Max Balkan to leave the home where derision from his mother and sister comes in "torrents," because despite his lofty daydreams he has no life apart from that atmosphere. His boyhood construction of an elegant sailboat in the basement objectifies, along with his incompetence, the inescapability of the Ripple Street tenement: he cannot get the boat through the doorway (41). In *Low Company* it does occur to Herbert Lurie to leave Neptune Beach in disgust. For him the option of escape is real: he has the money to rent a flat on the treelined Eastern Parkway, with its symbol of culture, the Museum of Art. But though the community at Ann's is not his actual family, he returns for reasons that are evidently similar to Philip's.

In American literary tradition the use of collective identity is most closely associated with Whitman. But whereas his approach and ideology are celebratory, another tendency developed later in American letters, using collective portraits to dramatize disenchantment with the American promise. Little heard of today, the first American realistic novelist who wrote in the Naturalist or necessitarian ideology, Edgar Watson Howe (1856–1937), uses the multicharacter structure in *The Story of a Country Town* (1888), a novel about a bleak midwestern neighborhood. Howe supports his elegiac mood through the cumulative pessimistic effect of the various plots. Howe's dour picture, according to S. J. Sackett, prepared readers for Edgar Lee Masters's *Spoon River Anthology,* Sherwood Anderson's *Winesburg, Ohio,* and Sinclair Lewis's *Main Street.*[8]

The documentary technique that gives a cross section of society is at the center of American realism. Not only Norris in his wheat stories, but also Howells in *A Hazard of New Fortunes,* with the city of New York the focus of attention, and James in *The Bostonians* use the cross-section technique. This plural protagonism gained strength after 1929 and became more an instrument of social consciousness when writers of stature like Theodore Dreiser, Edmund Wilson, and John Steinbeck toured the nation's suffering regions to write documentary narratives on the effects of the economic miasma. *In Dubious Battle,* even more than *The Grapes of Wrath,* distributes its focus for social purposes. John Dos Passos, in such works as *Three Soldiers,* multiplies his protagonists to attack the mystique of honor in World War I, and in *Manhattan Transfer* shows the evil of commercialism through the city as protagonist. The device of plural protagonism which Fuchs adopts in order to balance conflicting sympathies has for the most part served rather to advance the "adequate induction" of writers' beliefs.

The multiple-protagonist technique became popular among writers of drama as well in the 1920s and 1930s as a means of representing oppression. Elmer Rice's *Street Scene,* Sidney Kingsley's *Dead End,* with its thirty-three characters—many of them nameless—and "a crowd," as well as Clifford Odets's plays, especially *Awake and Sing!* and *Paradise Lost,* exemplify the collective picture of struggling immigrants who are defeated in America.

While Fuchs was writing his first novel, about the time when characterization of the group as a social weapon was increasing in American literature, the delayed release in this country of Joyce's *Ulysses* introduced a prodigious balancing influence in the direction of ambiguity; Joyce's use of the split protagonist is still acknowledged as the most highly achieved in literature. In American fiction of this century, however, the ambiguities of *Winesburg, Ohio* most closely suggest the subgenre of plural protagonist in which Fuchs works: the portrayal of the thwarted need for love within a microcosmic community.

Fuchs becomes a master of plot in *Low Company,* whereas Anderson's strengths lie elsewhere than in plot, yet the two writers encounter similar problems in form which are related to their philosophy of uncertainty. This uncertainty governs their treatment of materialistic values as being alarming without their concentrating on institutions or character types. Wright Morris's comment on Anderson applies as well to Fuchs: "Alienation and estrangement, various forms of emotional and intellectual malnutrition" that would become a commonplace in American fiction, are never *common* in Anderson. "Each man suffers his own, and we cannot conceive the character without it."[9]

Fuchs manages to make his philosophy of uncertainty compatible with parody, even though parody, like all forms of satire, has always been a moral weapon. He lessens the claims of sympathy made by his array of characters through devices like parody that place distance between reader and character. At the same time, much of the energy of his fiction is produced by the contradiction between the assumed maturity shared by parodist and reader on the one hand and a skepticism about assumptions on the other. The position that nothing can be assumed, which is the basis, according to Maurice Charney, of the interrogative mode of Jewish comedy,[10] seems a logical response to the demands of integrating two disparate cultures, the European Jewish town and the heterogeneous American metropolis. Fuchs undermines his own undermining; he dampens the normative function of parody with a fluidity of perspectives that conveys the dynamic of questioning. In *Summer in Williamsburg,* for example, one of a group of old Jewish men studying the Talmud reads aloud:

> "Rabbi ben Onz said this is to mean this, Rabbi ben Twoz, of a later generation, said it is to mean that, while here, nearer to our own time, Rabbi ben Threez said that in spite of the opinions of these venerated rabbis, it means neither this nor that, but, if the word 'fourz' is properly understood, the passage clearly means part of this and part of that together but neither this nor that in themselves, but in part, together and also the other thing added."

Various men, after deliberating, respond with "Hichle," "Pichle," and "Schmichle," and finally Old Miller, Philip's sage, pronounces, "Hichle, Pichle, Schmichle," and interprets the Good Book as saying, "Va-cha-choo-loo, va-cha-choo-loo," or, "when the wind will blow, the cradle will rock" (50–51). One critic cites this passage as a rude satire of the representatives of Orthodoxy.[11] But the ridiculing is followed a few lines after by an exaltation of the old men, which is itself called into question in turn:

> Oh, these mysterious men in their black, shiny caftans, in their skull caps, these old men who come together in the evenings to play tick-tack-toe with the great Talmud, itself brought down miraculously through the centuries. In our time we must admire and respect this fervor, this tradition. They are true heroes in a world of puppets and therefore we do not understand them. These old men who find synagogues in a tenement basement store with the terrible toilets facing the back yards. These old men nodding over the yellow, holy-odored volumes, arguing in a straight line of tradition that extends over the

world in width, in depth to the earliest times, in length to God himself.
What dimensions, what awful dimensions, what wonderful men as
they spit generously on the dirty floor. (P. 51)

The warring in this passage between its parody and its homage is
characteristic of Fuchs in the way that it shows the testing of
vantage points.

Fuchs consistently works with perspective in mind. In *Summer
in Williamsburg* Philip occasionally behaves in a manner that em-
barrasses him, as when he bitterly describes to Ruth the ugliness of
Williamsburg. "Where I live the view is hidden by garbage cans and
boys swinging dead cats by their tails at tourists who come slum-
ming. Do you mind sewer smells? They're terrible, but good for your
soul" (275). Reflecting afterwards on his tendency to melodrama,
Philip becomes part of the carnival from which he is always "collecting." At the lighthouse at Sandy Hook, where the physical
distance makes automobiles, railroads, and ocean liners look like
pictures painted on vases, he and Ruth meet the keeper's son, a
magnificent blond boy on whose face "was the unconscious ease of
being that has a kinship with the sea, the wind, and the sky." When
the boy comes upon the pair kissing and asks what Philip is doing to
Ruth, Philip's typically wry response is, "What's the matter? Don't
you go to the movies here?" (276). The lighthouse visit reminds
Philip how removed he is from natural simplicity, while it reminds
the reader how close to it Philip is.

In *Homage to Blenholt* Fuchs most conspicuously employs the
telegraphic montage, or abrupt and incongruous switch from one
scene to another, to form an impression of indeterminacy, or what
Tzvetan Todorov calls "undecidability."[12] This technique is akin to
Eliot's in "The Waste Land." An illustration of this process is the
shift from Max Balkan as he listens to *La Bohème,* his tears trick-
ling down into his ears, to the conversation among the "hired
cutthroats," Thickneck, Firpo, Amchy, and Pip (211). The bathos of
Max's grief for himself is intensified next to the talk among
Blenholt's mourners of their (surgical) operations, their sinus troubles, and the Dodgers. Firpo's worried question to Thickneck, "You
believe there's a life after death?" is answered by, "Aw . . . shad-
dap. You're worse than my sinus trouble" (213).

A major value of this scene is the thugs' corroboration of the
heroic vision for which Max grieves. They recall not only the
sixteen-cylinder Cadillac but also "the sense of high-handed adventure that [Blenholt] brought to their lives, the glorious splendor and
their feats of valor and daring. While he lived they could feel

powerful and strong." Thickneck says softly to his comrades, "You know, fellows, Blenholt was a regular king" (216). The equivocal rhetoric of this montage is characteristic of Fuchs: it simultaneously emphasizes Max's self-pity and justifies his sense of loss.

The final line of *Homage to Blenholt* provides another instance of this ambiguity of perspective. From the novel's opening conversation between Max and Ali Baba, Max's inventiveness is his most engaging quality. At the conclusion Label Balkan contemplates his son's surrender of his imagination to the world's demands, a surrender that evokes his own. Adjusting the shoulder straps of the advertising signs he wears, Label acknowledges Max's spiritual death. "It seemed to the old man that this death of youth was among the greatest tragedies in experience and that all the tears in America were not enough to bewail it." Label's reflection is not the final word, however. The narrator concludes, "But all the same the evening sun that day went down on time" (302). The emotional drop from immense significance to utter insignificance in the scheme of things draws the reader's attention not only to the Balkans' self-dramatizing propensity but also to the elusiveness of a perspective that encompasses both final truths.

Commentators on Fuchs's novels and stories, in concentrating on his acute powers of observation, have disregarded his use of symbols; only one image has received much attention as a symbol—the butterfly in the subway that Philip and his friend Charles watch with wonder in the first novel and that Munves describes in the second.[13] But there are other important symbols in the novels. Aside from the motif of falling, which will be dealt with in the chapter on *Homage to Blenholt,* Fuchs works with two main emblems of the problematics of perspective. In *Homage to Blenholt* doors and in *Low Comedy* mirrors convey the ambiguities of spatial position.

The importance of doors in the second novel lies in the absence of privacy, and consequently perspective, in the tenement community. Mrs. Balkan asks, "What do you want to talk in private?" (68). Cramped space is accountable for some of this condition, as in the telephone conversations that Rita must share with her mother and in the Balkans' sleeping arrangements, Mrs. Balkan and Rita in the bedroom, Max and Mr. Balkan on a daybed in the living room. But space does not account for all of it: Ruth meets Max at his mailbox and demands to read his correspondence. Intrusion is the general style. A strange old peddler enters flats without knocking and manages each time to spoil a crucial moment. The cleaning lady, too, assumes the privilege.

The door opened and Mrs. Wohl marched in with her mop and dust cloths. Munves and Rita stopped.

"Dancing?" Mrs. Wohl asked, beaming at the sight. "Dance, dance, children. Don't let me stop you."

"Mrs. Wohl," Rita said severely, "you got a door in your house?"

"Sure, I have a door. What a question. Who hasn't a door in America?"

"Do people walk in without knocking in your house too?"

Mrs. Wohl turned and rapped on the door with her mop. "All right," she said pleasantly. "Now I knocked." (P. 143)

The two words

"The Door"

stand like a chapter heading alone in the center of a line on page 285 and again on 286. They frame the description of the scene that Max, returning with the mesh bag of onions, knows awaits him in the apartment. "Behind it were Mr. Balkan, Mrs. Balkan, Rita, Ruth, Munves, the world," with its hum and buzz of expectation. After the second

"The Door"

Max opens it and enters. "He had to." Replying to their questions with "Nothing," he receives "the torrents," "battering him, bruising, smashing," until he excuses himself and retreats to the bathroom. "Protected and hidden by the bathroom door," Max turns on both faucets full force and reads a clipping with a Horatio Alger message pasted inside the door of the medicine chest. He recalls his meeting with Mr. Atwater with hatred, until he hears his father calling "Maxie. Maxie." "The door again" (291).

When he emerges Max is a changed person, resigned to any dreary employment in order to become normal and serve this crowd. He goes into the bedroom to tell Ruth that "he surrendered, he would get a job, they would get married. He felt cold now, with no trace of tears for himself. That was all over. Balkan felt himself a man" (293).

Another figurative use Fuchs makes of doors, in a scene involving Rita, illustrates the epistemological function of his multiple-perspective technique. Rita bangs the apartment door shut (129) and leaves the reader to the conversation between the Balkans. Four pages later, precisely the same banging-shut of the door is repeated, only this time with the perspective changed, as Rita arranges her clothing and expression in the hallway before entering Munves's apartment—without knocking. Time is reversed to the first telling of her exit, and Rita watches her parents from Munves's window, as they hold the conversation which the narrative has just recounted, in the room where she has just left them. "There was her mother taking it out on Pop just as though it was a silent moving picture." As she grows enraged at her mother's nagging, Munves watches her in the same way, "spying at her out of the corner of his eyes as his scalp shivered . . . at the preoccupation in her expression. What a strange girl!" Fuchs distributes credibility among the characters by the shift from Rita's to Munves's view in the same paragraph, together with the shift from one side of the door to the other, and from Mrs. Balkan's haranguing within the flat to her pantomime observed through the window. Rita's distress, in particular, complicates her shrillness. The epistemological value of this whole passage is in its casting of doubt on the validity of any single perception.

The basement door which barred the emergence of Max's glorious sailboat when he was younger (41) epitomizes the constriction of the tenements, but it also reveals, among other things, Max's ridiculous limitedness in not having taken practical facts into account. In *Homage to Blenholt* no character's judgment is given sustained weight, the three friends and Label Balkan being discredited by their eccentricities. The experiences of the group are observed prismatically; even their senses of one another's selves shift, as in Munves's description of his friend Max, first as an idealist, then as not an idealist. The three friends are capable only of such half-truths as Munves's remark that "the characteristic of genius . . . is the quality of not being understood" (219). These multiple partial views convey a metaphysics that renounces any voice, including the parodic, as representing certainty.

Fuchs plays with relative perspectives in *Low Company* also, in the scene in which Shorty and Madame Pavlovna are watching a moving picture about a woman who performs on the stage. Gazing at the gorgeous blonde on the screen who brings ruin to men, Shorty is absorbed in his own greater drama as Sophia rebuffs him for pinching her thigh. He composes his scenario:

> Here he had gone out of his way to show the lonely widow a good time; here he had been stood up once; he had forgiven her, had taken her out for supper and a show, spent money like water, and the first

move he made was purposely minunderstood and she got sore. B'gee!
(P. 222)

While these two movie spectators provide a frame for the play-within-a-play, they become a spectacle themselves when Shorty's bragging upsets the man sitting behind him. Meanwhile, the profound distress of two other members of the audience, Karty and Arthur, after the killing of Louis Spitzbergen, dwarfs the crisis on the screen.

The most unsettling questions Fuchs evokes in *Low Company* about perceived appearances are present in his portrayal of Shubunka, an ugly man absorbed with his image in the mirror. While Shubunka appears to others and himself as monstrous, "like an ape," he lives in a mirrored apartment and looks at mirrors at every opportunity. The first section that deals with Shubunka begins and ends with his looking at a mirror.

> The telephone rang. Shubunka placed the tweezers at his side on the bedspread but he kept on looking into the mirror, gravely studying his face. Gradually his features broke into a warm-hearted benign smile. His eyes solemnly examined his appearance to see how he looked with that expression on his face. The smile disappeared, his face grew reflective and soft, the lips parting a little. The bell rang again. Shubunka now was glaring into the mirror, his brow raised in furrows above the fierce bulging eyes, his teeth showing. Solemnly his eyes noted the expression in the glass. Then his face broke, the angry lines merging into those of a man who has just been amused, at first mildly. But now the joke grows, his cheeks go higher on the bones, the grin grows wider, wider, bursting into uproarious laughter. Shubunka's diaphragm shook and his eyes teared. The bell was still ringing. (Pp. 55–56)

When the cashier at Ann's refuses his wedding gift of cash, Shubunka, his expression "full of hurt and pity for himself," leaves the shop "[looking] at the wall mirror to catch a glimpse of his face when it showed sorrow" (65–66). When his phone calls to pool parlors and candy stores fail to turn up any "boys" to help him deal with the syndicate,

> A shadow of perplexity clouded his face. Shubunka, in his wonder, took the time to study his expression in the mirror, watching the slow doubt deepen in his face. "I do not understand," he said softly to the mirror. "I cannot understand. Where could they [his hoodlums] all be?" (P. 88)

In the absence of mirrors he takes comfort against fear by envisioning his appearance "in his mind's eye . . . , as though he were looking at himself in a mirror" (90), or by taking his reflection where he finds it:

> Feeling so sorry for himself that actual tears came to his eyes, the fat man looked intently into the greasy enameled table top to see if he could discern the appearance of his face in the dim reflection. (P. 93)

When his life is in peril Shubunka stops to "[sneak] the view of his profile, full length," in the triple mirrors of Lurie's dress shop (144). Fuchs may be playing a dark joke, similar to O'Neill's about the iceman's coming, by having Shubunka's father a glazier.[14] In any event, the mirror is an objective correlative to Shubunka's masochistic self-consciousness: "Outside, men lay in wait for him, he faced ruin and death, but he was composed and resigned, a man going to his just end. The image of himself in his mind's eye soothed him" (254).

More than Max Balkan's odd gait, described in the opening lines of *Homage to Blenholt,* Shubunka's waddling on his broken legs (variously called bent or bowed) is used as an emblem of his limitedness and his doom. Though the accident which caused Shubunka's disability may recall the fatal fall of Fuchs's brother, just as likely a source is a novel which Fuchs admired, Michael Gold's *Jews Without Money,* in which the young protagonist's father, a house painter, falls from a scaffold and breaks every bone in his legs. This mishap in the Gold novel epitomizes the failures of the heroic family that prompt the young man to espouse communism.[15] With Shubunka as neither villain nor hero, his deformity underscores both the pathos of his struggles and the plausibility of his failure. That the lame sufferer should also be the panderer is the hallmark of Fuchs's tone.

Besides his repulsive appearance, Shubunka, Fuchs's most finely wrought character, has an unappealing personality. Readers have remarked on how disagreeable Fuchs's characters are in general, both in physical and personal traits. This observation assuredly holds true for *Low Company,* in which the most sympathetic of the major figures, Herbert and Arthur, have few attractive qualities. The reader becomes closely acquainted with a whoremonger; an obsessive gambler, thief, and finally killer; and a real-estate baron who begrudges water to a distraught woman and declares her sobs "not good for business" (216). The women are all unappealing: knock-kneed Bella Karty is awkward and robotlike; Ann, a hypochondriac, rationalizes her husband's role in the degrading of other women by the need to make a profit; and Madame Pavlovna, before being assaulted by Shorty, changes into a black chiffon negligee to lecture him on Platonic love. Many of the characters are fat and bulky with faces "like slabs of meat," or sickly; Karty is referred to as a weasel and Shorty as a cockroach.

Fuchs's portrayals are an invitation to the reader to deny the characters the compassion that they deny one another. His stylized rendering withholds even the relief of a gracious or genuinely pious neighbor. The reader can with little hesitation bless an Emma Woodhouse or a David Copperfield, but the fools and reprobates whom Fuchs makes multidimensional place the reader in a position to question his or her own capacity for mercy. Because of Fuchs's view of comprehensiveness as one's only hope of comprehending, *Low Company,* in continually shifting its bases of certainty, may be seen as turning its portrait into a mirror.

Fuchs waits until late in the novel, when Shubunka is desolate in his room after being warned to leave town, to disclose to the reader the fat man's childhood of extreme poverty, abhorrent living conditions, a disabling fall, and a waddling body that elicited undisguised scorn and horror. Shubunka has striven for the prestige that would force respect from the other people at Ann's, aware that nothing will earn their affection. That information in the reader's possession wars with the ugliness of Shubunka's business. Fuchs works his balances in this scene with much at stake: he develops Shubunka's exaggerated self-consciousness; his sudden rise in hopes after the sniffler's phone call; his rush to get to Ann's to settle for working as the new boss's "collector"; his fortunate fall when a bullet rings out; and his despondency greater than his terror when he discovers that the sniffler's friendliness was feigned. A revolting figure, his hair excessively pomaded and his mouth slobbering, a man who trades on women as merchandise, the fat man is nevertheless the object of pursuit by killers. Human in his ambiguous sincerity, Shubunka must, without sentimentality—in the terms of the epigraph—unharden the reader's heart. If that happens the reader promises an end to the circle; if it does not, Fuchs's point remains more excruciatingly valid. The "low" of the title finally assesses the reader's capacity to know another's feelings when, finally, Fuchs invites us to see beyond the stage of Neptune Beach.

Before [Shubunka] lay the houses, and stretching in front of them was Brooklyn, the city and the world. Within the darkened buildings were people sleeping, thousands and thousands, and there was not one

among them who had heart for him, who even knew of his despair or
would come to his aid. Spread out before him lay the world hardened
and unfeeling, black as the night itself. Where could Shubunka go?
(P. 270)

Withholding from the reader a full identification with his young
artist in the first novel, and with his grotesques in the second, in
Low Company Fuchs shows most clearly through his play of competing sympathies that his elusive approach to his material is an
attempt not to evade but rather to encompass truth.

4
Summer in Williamsburg

In his fictionalized chronicle of the section of Brooklyn where he spent his boyhood,[1] Fuchs confronts the possibilities of objectivity claimed for the naturalist approach to writing. The novel's key word and activity, "collect," introduced by Philip Hyman's mentor Old Miller, parodies Zola's empirical ideology. The laboratory metaphor that gives the novel its strongest naturalistic element is presented derisively through Miller's unreliability as a sage and the unproductiveness of his method. Playing upon the limited interpretations of Philip, Fuchs merges naturalistic subject matter and modernist method, offering and withdrawing patterns of completion as part of a larger pattern of irresolution.

Like Sherwood Anderson, Fuchs has been critically assailed for failing either to search for patterns of order through myths or ideologies, or to provide, in Brom Weber's words about Anderson, "descriptions of objects and behavior that possessed the irreducible precision of scientific writing."[2] While Fuchs attends to the grim scenic details that manifest impersonal socioeconomic forces, he limits the magnitude of these forces in favor of the mystery of human motivations. The empirical collecting that is his frame of reference in *Summer in Williamsburg* also includes lyrical speculations on the mystery of God—as another chronicler.

The conspicuous chronicler within Fuchs's chronicle is Philip Hayman, who, like Sherwood Anderson's George Willard in *Winesburg, Ohio,* is seeking answers. George says, "I must get myself into touch with something orderly and big." Philip, prompted by the suicide of an apparently content neighbor, strains to comprehend the world order according to which such a person would choose to end his life. He goes to the wisest man he knows, Old Miller, who instructs him to collect observations scientifically. A miser and wife-beater for whom the only truth and meaning in life is money, "the sage in the long beard" counsels Philip to make a laboratory out of Williamsburg: "You must pick [it] to pieces until you have them all spread out on your table before you, a dictionary of Williamsburg." Man, he says, as the product of the commingling of millions of psychical atoms, "therefore moves mysteriously, but he is a scientific outcome of cause and effect" (12). Denying the existence of beauty in such impersonal phenomena as the ocean and the moon, Miller tells Philip that people move about "in the dinginess immersing themselves continuously in a sedative warm bath of ideals and dreams, but these [are] artificial and delusory as a soft waltz" (10). Taking in Miller's words, Philip tallies an inventory of his material, which includes "that couple, fat and perspiring, in holiday clothes with bathing-suit bags at their sides, drinking vanilla soda water at the candy stand," and "Yosowitz' laundry with the curtains stretched on the tall racks as they dry in the sun." While he mentally prepares to "collect and analyze" the procession of humanity that comes down the street, Philip, passing by the dark window of a funeral parlor, "turned his head to observe his appearance in the glass as he walked" (13–14). Fuchs makes it clear here and elsewhere that Philip, as a participant in the universal grotesquerie, is not a privileged interpreter of it. While his analytical powers arm him against sentimental excesses of spontaneous tenderness, they do not suffice to raise him out of the general bewilderment.

Mainly through Philip, Fuchs probes the possibilities of Miller's/Zola's empiricism and finds it wanting; Philip's complexly tender feelings towards his father, for example, are unaccountable through Miller's contemplation of millions of atoms. Fuchs jokes with the technique of a comprehensive inventory by using it in his overview—through the character of God—of the community which includes Philip. Fuchs's dissatisfaction with received notions is expressed in his God's being a mildly interested observer of human exigencies, benignly disposed but powerless. Two glimpses of God, early and late in the novel, are consistent with Fuchs's pattern of exploring truths about Williamsburg and humanity through an inclusiveness of perspectives. The first of these glimpses occurs while Philip is at the movies.

> High up, a million miles into the sky, God sits on a big cloud. He looks absent-mindedly about. His beard is long and very white, the flesh of His face is gnarled. Now He peers down and for a moment His gaze rests on Williamsburg and He says to Himself, How are things going down there, I wonder? . . . God wonders and looks. Everything is just as it always has been and as it will be. Mrs. Linck's flesh moves in rhythm to the count of the rocker while the guinea pigs scurry beneath her. Papravel wears a derby. (P. 47)

After observing Miller, Cohen, and Mahler, somewhat as Philip tries to observe them, God turns his attention to Philip himself, who, "with a half-conscious expression is gazing at Gloria Swanson" (48). Fuchs places the reader in an intimacy with God beyond the awareness of Philip, a twenty-year-old writer still in his note-taking stage.

In the later passage, too, God collects from "high up a million miles into the sky."

> God wonders and looks. Everything is just as it always has been and as it will be. . . . Mrs. Linck moves in heavy rhythm to the count of the rocker while the guinea pigs explore the dinginess for scraps of food. On Papravel's head rests a derby. (P. 358)

God looks down and observes small changes, the absence now of Sussman and Miller, the activities of young Yetta, Natie, and Davey, and the private moments of Mahler, Yenta Maldick, Tessie, and Cohen. "As for Philip, God looks down and sees him too, and He says, is that fellow still pondering at the window? He's like a bird standing up on one leg all the time" (359). God takes inventory just as Philip does, of sunny Ripple Street, the stables, the curtains stretched for drying in front of Yosowitz's laundry, and the housewives with their baby carriages. But by making Philip one of the observed, Fuchs achieves what Philip does elsewhere when he calls authors liars who use selectivity to presume divine judgment: the novelist, like the character, suggests that what he is trying to express is ineffable. Philip repeats Miller's theory several times near the novel's conclusion. But it has not served him at all, and the refrain grows increasingly ironic.

> "Men are the sum of a million infinitesimal phenomena and experiences. A million atoms of a certain type produce, in the end, wood just as a million of another make stone and iron and gold. The same is true of these men. . . . If you would really discover the reason for people's actions you must pick Williamsburg to pieces until you have them all spread out before you on your table, a dictionary of Williamsburg." (Pp. 374–75)

When the reader last sees Philip, the young man is again recalling Miller's words, this time after his mother tells him of the discovery of one of the Sussman babies in the river. "That means they're all found now," he observes as a scientist. His mother replies, "Yes, but what good does that do anybody?" (379) Philip, grappling with cause and effect, immediately recalls the sage's clinical methodology for learning reasons, but his reference to "cold wisdom" suggests his consciousness of irony. He goes to his dinner "waiting for the years to come to see what would happen to him" (379). Fuchs's placement of Philip beneath a greater scrutinizing eye extends that irony: God's powers of observation also produce nothing. The only agent for good in Williamsburg is the compassion that motivates Mrs. Hayman.

It is a mistake, then, to identify Philip with the author, or even to regard him as the novel's sole protagonist. While the story's preoccupation with love, death, and making a living is appropriate material for a twenty-year-old central character, and *Summer in Williamsburg* seems a conventionally structured story about a young man's deepest struggles, Philip's centrality is diminished by his sharing of the role of collector with other characters, including God, all of whom are incapable of embracing the totality. As Philip says, "To present a man honestly you would really have to give him entire" (374).

Fuchs does more himself than collect. With Philip only part of the Williamsburg panorama, Fuchs's gentle discrediting of the prospective writer as his spokesman is consistent with the notion that both Philip and Fuchs express about ineffability. The novel presents a dramatized network of questions, and the problems of the literary artist are a vital part of the mystery it addresses. The questions are not only Philip's—about why Sussman took his life, or what to do about Papravel's tempting offer, or even how to be an honest craftsman—but also Fuchs's—about adequately representing Philip-in-Williamsburg. All of these questions remain unanswered except the last, which is answered by the novel itself as an entity. To shape such a coherent entity Fuchs must behave as semidivine selector and arranger, very like Thackeray, whom Philip reads with wonder and accusations. Assuming that responsibility tentatively, Fuchs does what he can to cast doubt on the power of the imagination to comprehend experience, mostly by emphasizing the incompleteness of individual perspectives.

Of the three formidable sources of Philip's bewilderment—the subjects of death, of love, and of making a living—Fuchs's treatment of the third is discussed in Chapter 2 of this study. Though love receives more attention, the uses of both death and love are organic to the novel. The self-inflicted death by gas of Philip's neighbor Mr. Sussman, who was employed and appeared robust and content, followed the next day by another suicide in the neighborhood, precipitates Philip's metaphysical inquiries that thread the novel. The mystery of Mrs. Sussman's emotional collapse and suicide/infanticide after returning unmarried from Montana brings the novel to its close. That these events finally remain mysteries is consistent with Fuchs's themes of indeterminacy and the limits to the artist's controlling vision. Aside from demonstrating the fragility of the Sussmans' ostensibly successful marriage, their violent deaths frame the novel's events and point up the incomprehensibility of those events. Miller is both correct and incorrect. It is at the same time useful and futile to study the behavior of man as an organism of cause and effect.

Love is the other mystery which occupies Philip, and the subject which draws Fuchs closer to naturalism than any other. *Summer in Williamsburg* contains an assortment of the love and sexual relationships possible between men and women; while Philip's involvements with Tessie and Ruth Kelman receive substantial attention, his story is only part of the novel's variations on the theme of the hopeless climate for love in Williamsburg.

Along with the multiple protagonists, Philip, Harry, Cohen, and Davey, as discussed in Chapter 3 of this study, Fuchs uses the community as a collective protagonist to display Williamsburg's grim prospects for tender emotions. Use of the community as protagonist allows him to expose three aspects at once: a range of personalities as diverse as Mr. Hayman and Papravel, the dynamics between those personalities, and the process by which both the personalities and the dynamics develop. Beliefs about love, for example, represented in the Lincks and in the children, Davey and Yetta, suggest the politicization of sexuality as part of a Williamsburg education. Davey misses an appointment with Yetta because of a street fight, but she rejects that excuse: "Tell me, David, . . . is a street fight more important than our love?" (221). His sweet feelings yield to a new toughness, the thrill-seeking and swagger of other hangers-on at Cheap Simon's candy store: "Who did she think she was anyway? . . . What is love? A load of crap" (296). Yetta in turn flirts with Davey's friend Natie the Buller and belittles Davey. Fuchs comes his closest to naturalism in showing, through the dynamics between Davey, Yetta, and Natie, the early engendering of sexuality as power.

Philip applies a scientific lens to life's laboratory, in order not only to gain knowledge but even more to survive emotionally. He must first survive the lesser shock of Tessie's choosing to marry Schlausser, then the greater hurt of losing Ruth. But although both these disappointments result from economic causes, Philip, rather than a naturalist observer, is the novel's custodian of nineteenth-century romantic values about family, home, and love. Fuchs, meanwhile, achieves his own skeptical tone comprehensively, not through Philip's youthfully cynical remarks but through the syntax of scenes which is cumulatively more telling than their respective content.

Philip, the novel's most perspicacious character, points out the delusory devices of his friends Tessie and Cohen to escape from the costs of attachment. Yet he is conscious, when he yields himself to the trap of romantic feelings, that they "[leave] me open for a fine kick in the pants" (220), and he manufactures "consolation in advance" (274) for the inevitable loss of Ruth Kelman. His friend Cohen regards Philip's detachment as too successful. He accuses Philip of escaping from life by the mental habit of "withdrawal and bystanding" (356). Nevertheless, Philip's efforts to be "philosophical" serve him little (300), and his heartbreak over Ruth is substantial (324).

The need to escape which afflicts all the other characters in some form afflicts Philip too, as he tries to avoid risking everything. But Philip is twenty and full of resources to help ready himself to survive losing Ruth. The other characters possess feebler weapons for escaping from insignificance and loss. Sam Linck's answer to powerlessness is infidelity, Cohen's is a host of fantasies, and Harry's is a feigned insouciance. And as the violent disappearance of the Sussmans demonstrates, the force of affection collapses under the despair of tenement culture.

Not surprisingly for the thirties, Fuchs depicts more mechanisms of escape available to his male than to his female characters. Philip, although he is the novel's primary collector, is nevertheless excluded from most of the novel's observations of women's unhappiness, including Tessie's. The waste and desolation of these women's lives and their helplessness to change matters is the stuff of naturalism, and the women's disagreeableness demonstrates how fully the tenement culture is within them. The economic woes that restrict men's alternatives in the novel bear even more on the women, as the early saga of Mrs. Linck's three daughters illustrates. Two of the daughters have become burlesque dancers and one is a prostitute. If a young woman in Williamsburg does not marry someone with means and kindness, her life is miserable; in order to marry well she must have good looks and something everyone calls luck. The Lincks, as Sam says of himself, have terrible luck.

In Sam's mistress Marge, Fuchs provides a more complete picture of a woman crushed by the social structure. She is an eighteen-year-old who depends on men to avoid starvation. Sam's economic power over her seems to enhance the piquancy of their relationship for him, along with exchanges of insults. Marge's waitress job is so insecure that she is fired after Sam creates a scene in the restaurant where she works. Possessed of even fewer illusions about love than Sam, Marge hires thugs to beat him up when she loses her job, but then returns to his abuses.

Tessie, Philip's longtime companion, is not much luckier than Marge. Despairing of Philip's practical possibilities, Tessie marries Abe Schlausser, a traveling salesman and substantial provider whom she finds repulsive. Perhaps Fuchs's most gripping domestic description is of Tessie desperately creating a romantic atmosphere to welcome her bridegroom Schlausser back from a business trip. Arching and posturing before a threeway mirror she drapes a Spanish shawl to make her look like a senorita in a calendar picture, and resolves to please her hard-working husband with "her gentleness, her culture, and her beauty" (301).

> She strode out of the room with her arms outstretched to seize his hands. But the sight of Schlausser somewhat unnerved her. . . . She had almost forgotten he was such a short-sized man. He had loosened his collar on account of the heat. It was wilted and curled at the ends. Behind the brass collar button the unshaved hair of his throat stuck out against the moist whiteness. It was a little ugly.
> "My, my," he said with enthusiasm. "What a lady I married. I never saw such a pretty one. Aren't you going to kiss me?"
> "Of course," Tessie said, and gave him her cheek. (P. 303)

After dinner Schlausser surveys the softly lit living room. "He looked at the piano, the etchings on the wall, and the furniture. It was all his. He owned it, together with his refined wife" (303). Finding him greasy and repugnant, Tessie defers sex by playing Mendelssohn on the piano, her face "sad and intense with the music." Meanwhile, "Schlausser smoked his cigar, satisfied and completely content because his home-coming had been so carefully welcomed. She had taken care of every detail, the lights, the dinner, and now the piano. What a pretty picture she made, with the piano lid in the air" (305–6). In this remarkably comical yet sad scene Fuchs particularizes the consequences of sexual contracts built on practical exigencies alone.

Without either cancelling or excusing his women characters' disagreeable qualities, Fuchs underscores the absurdity of the options forced on them. After Anna Linck and Marge engage in a violent streetfight over Sam, the wry comment of the narrative voice is, "This was what they had been fighting over" (97). Anna, contending with both Sam and his mother, whose apartment they share, grows more desolate as the novel progresses. She suffers especially keenly on account of a catastrophic vacation she spends with her children at a mountain resort, an event which is a synecdoche for her life. At the resort Anna's inability to control her rage results in a physical battle with another woman, and her embarrassment at facing the others in the community afterwards takes priority over the marked improvement in her boys' health. Dragging them back prematurely to the sweltering city and discovering Sam together with Marge, she becomes more wretched than ever, because she is obliged to recognize that she has no leverage to obstruct her husband's affair and no alternative but to endure it (347).

Anna's lack of reflective powers and the contribution of her own meanspiritedness to her troubles prevent her from being simply a vehicle of social doctrine. These individual shortcomings undercut the naturalistic bent of the novel. But it is the characterization of Mrs. Hayman as a person who values kindness and service that most counters the naturalist impression. Fuchs's tone towards her is tender. Along with her husband, Mrs. Hayman is the inculcator of Philip's humane values within a squalid, cramped, and loveless community; unlike her husband, she seems to be happy, the only happy person in the novel. Fuchs keeps her from being too appealing by her occasional chiding of Mr. Hayman for being as "topsy-turvy" as the demented Yente Maldick. Yet she anticipates the second novel's more disagreeable Mrs. Balkan in only that quality.

Philip's mother knows what sorts of things to say to Old Miller on his deathbed, and throws herself into assisting the widow Sussman when she can hardly care for herself. Mrs. Hayman keeps herself busy and cares about her neighbors as if they were her own family; she enjoys her son's jokes at her expense, thinks that her gangster brother is not a bad fellow, and maneuvers around her husband's depressiveness. It appears that Mrs. Hayman enjoys the best that a woman in Fuchs's Williamsburg can hope for, the opportunity to nurture others, a sense of humor, and tranquillity in her personal life, though in the intimacy of the tenement it is difficult to distinguish what is personal. Set off against Mrs. Hayman's force for good, Old Miller's theory of atomic causes and effects appears hollow.

The two married couples in *Summer in Williamsburg* who appear to have sustained some measure of affection and good will—elements absent from marriages in the other two Brooklyn novels—are the Sussmans and the Haymans. What has gone awry for the Sussmans is Philip's abiding puzzle, an aspect of life's essential incomprehensibility. The other couple's retention of ideal values is another mystery, one that further restricts the novel's naturalist tendencies.

The Haymans are not introduced until page 59 and are not given close attention until Philip's return from Havers Falls. The reader becomes acquainted with the appealing elements of Philip's home and parents (after page 174) only after becoming engaged in the dilemma that both the Hayman sons face: the temptation of money as an escape, but Papravel's dirty means of acquiring it. Philip's disdain for the idyllic countryside and his eager return to the garbage and dead cats of the tenement make sense only because of the home his parents create. His fondness for both of them and his admiration for his father provide him with a base of strength that blesses no other character in Fuchs's oeuvre. They also make life difficult for Philip in that a lapse in integrity is a betrayal of them.

Moved by death's mysteriousness and looking for an order by which to make sense of it and live in spite of it, Philip seeks advice from Old Miller because the man whom he most admires, his father, no longer searches or strives. Mr. Hayman, aware that his advocacy for integrity is anachronistic, has no methodology for accommodating to the new world. Fuchs uses a parody of Sherwood Anderson to point up Philip's philosophical heritage from his father. Anderson amplifies the word "delicious" in describing the story of Dr. Reefy's marriage by means of the image of "the twisted little apples that grow in the orchards of Winesburg." After the crop has been picked and shipped away,

> On the trees are only a few gnarled apples that the pickers have rejected. . . . One runs from tree to tree over the frosted ground picking the gnarled, twisted apples and filling his pockets with them. Only the few know the sweetness of the twisted apples.[3]

Borrowing the image but inverting its theme, Fuchs has Mr. Hayman tell Philip, "People here [in America] remind me of the green, deformed, uneatable apples you find in a neglected orchard. No taste. No character" (243). As much as Philip admires his father, he must look elsewhere for some means of dealing with the present and savoring life.

Fuchs comments on relationships between men and women in the Williamsburg society by the device of montage—with the traveling glimpses of the characters patterned, not random.[4] Aside from the war that Philip's uncle wages for control of the resort bus company, these glimpses deal mostly with expectations and disappointments concerning love, on the part of young and old, men and women, married and unmarried, faithful and unfaithful. Fuchs's arrangement of scenes supplies more information than is available to Philip; the resulting triad of impressions suggests a perspective on Philip's own situation: that romantic love is fated to turn sour; that sex is usually trivial and brutal; and that young people become educated to betray not only others but also their own feelings of tenderness.

When Ruth Kelman, a girl from a prosperous family, enters the story and captivates Philip, Fuchs shifts on the same page (198) to Davey's delusions, "the gentle waltzes of his dreams" about a young woman named Susannah gliding toward him "down the country lane in white organdy"; this juxtaposition calls attention to the impracticality of Philip's attraction to Ruth. Philip's friend Charles later discloses that Dr. and Mrs. Kelman have their own sensible rules for the marriage of their daughter: "When a Kelman marries it's to a Rappaport, and vice-versa. That's how they keep the money in the family, I suppose" (323).

As forceful as the problem of income that subverts the sweetness of Fuchs's Williamsburg youths, time destroys whatever magic may have existed. Sam and Anna Linck married for love and not by arrangement, yet their marriage has become painful almost beyond endurance for them both. Sam arranges for Anna and the children to stay at a mountain resort, both of them using the children's benefit as the reason. When Sam takes them to the mountains, Anna speaks tearfully of how lonely she is. "They stood clumsily and didn't know how to kiss. The last time had been so long ago they felt as though kissing was nonsense and ridiculous, but now they knew they should be kissing each other good-bye and it was difficult to do it" (214). Sam pats her on the shoulder and leaves.

From the awkwardness of these two former lovers whose mutual imprisonment is so palpably rendered throughout the novel, Fuchs "cuts" to Philip and Ruth in blossoming love. That montage, by placing Philip's love story in a sobering perspective, makes Philip one of the collected more than a collector.

The relationship in Fuchs's first novel between the subject of love and the question of a controlling aspect is clearest in a scene dealing with literal perspective, the account of Philip's and Ruth's excursion to Sandy Hook, across the Bay in New Jersey's Atlantic Highlands. The scene, though brief, is important.[5] While much of the novel's material is the squalor proper to naturalistic treatment, the Sandy Hook setting is the novel's most romantic; yet the implications are more deterministic in this scene than in any other.

The scene directly follows one of Cohen's sad antics, in which he has just failed to effect a sexual relationship with the Communist woman, Shura. A taxi driver misconstrues Cohen's request to fix him up as a homosexual advance: " 'Are you making passes at me, dearie?' he said with a hard sweetness. 'Get the hell out of here before I slam my fist into your face' " (274). This episode of love-lessness and urban tawdriness is immediately followed by the most idyllic episode in Philip's life, an episode that is only momentarily freeing and that displays his thwarted capacities.

The first line after the break is Philip's question, "What is love?" Preparing himself, out of pride, to lose Ruth, he half-jokes to him-self: "A woman is nothing very important. Wife, mother, father, children, country, life, work, death—that's heroics, you get over it." As the steamer passes Brooklyn, Philip flaunts his cynicism by describing to Ruth the squalor that dooms their chances.

> "Where I live the view is hidden by garbage cans and boys swinging dead cats by their tails at tourists who come slumming. Do you mind sewer smells? They're terrible, but good for your soul. One must suffer. Through Purgatory to Paradise, like that guy Dostoievsky says. Some day I'll take you there and then you'll come back uplifted."
> (P. 275)

Philip's enchantment with Ruth, though understated, is evident, as she asks him why he is looking at her. " 'What's the matter?' she said anxiously. 'Is [my face] dirty?' 'No,' Philip said. What was the matter with him? 'You look very nice' " (275). His silent repeating of her question adequately suggests his vulnerability.

Unlike the Catskills, which Chaim's shoddy resort discloses to be a colony of Williamsburg, the New Jersey State Park at Sandy Hook, though less than fifteen miles away, is another world. For Philip, "Here it was wonderful." "After the dirty, sun-beaten streets of New York the quiet coolness and the blowing branches of the trees made them feel far away and refreshed." What the lovers see as they lie on the grassy hill near the lighthouse is the world in miniature. This change of aspect especially impresses Philip, whose collected images of Williamsburg are suffused with stifling close-ness. The lighthouse, which is in actuality eighty-five-feet high, has to seem a great height to a young man from the streets of Brooklyn. "The ocean liners, the toy railroad, the little automobiles from that distance gave an impression of unreality. . . . [like] the soft glazed colors and the dreamy pictures he had seen as a boy on hand-painted China vases." (275–76).

Chided by Ruth for being Russian-like in his seriousness, Philip characteristically replies by describing love in the same terms in which elsewhere he ponders the problem of fiction. "Love is like that. It has a beginning, a middle, and an end." Ruth, freer of cares than he, hints for and receives a kiss, which is interrupted by a stranger. "It was a blond boy. He was magnificent, his legs apart, looking down upon them with half a reprimand. . . . In all [Philip's] life he had never seen a boy like that. He did not belong to the earth. On his face was the unconscious ease of being that has a kinship with the sea, the wind, and the sky" (276). The lighthouse-keeper's son informs the pair of his family's custom of sharing whatever they find, and takes a piece of cake away with him. Philip takes away from the moment an unfamiliar exhilaration, a lifting of his Russian burden. "What was he worrying about? . . . There was no reason to hold back, he told himself, he could love Ruth without reserve, without worry, and without thought," and he gaily draws her shoulders to him (277).

The question "What is love?" that opens this three-and-a-half-page scene may not be answered, but it is dealt with. All that makes Ruth inaccessible to Philip slips into unimportance, like the automobiles grown tiny in the distance. All that shapes his proud cynicism too comes to appear distant. For the moment, Williamsburg ceases being the universe. Finally, the innocence of the blond boy throws Philip's bitter remarks into relief as a pose and allows his own innocence and capacity for simple pleasure to have its moment. Remote from home, parents, Papravel, and the tenement community, Sandy Hook—the complete name of which is Sandy Hook Life Saving Station[6]—gives Philip his only experience of being carefree, open, and able to risk loving, but the lifesaving is only for an afternoon. No other scene demonstrates so keenly the novel's play between hope and hopelessness, and no other scene so strongly conveys Philip's being molded by circumstance.

The theme of love touches the wider cast of characters, and, in two sections of the novel in particular, scenes that appear to be random form a cycle of plot-variations on that theme. Chapter 15 constitutes such a cycle. Following Anna Linck's calamities in the Catskills and the depiction of the want of tenderness in all the women and their marriages, the chapter portrays young Davey's sexual curiosity split from his tender feelings for Yetta; his initiation into manhood requires his removing himself both from love and his loved one. Hurt by a domestic misunderstanding with Yetta, Davey undertakes a ritual of manhood in feeling the breast of a promiscuous girl, Ida. Approaching Ida as an object involves more than Davey's setting aside the reveries Hollywood has inspired and shaped about fair womanhood in pastel organdy; he also sets aside the tremulous affection he experiences in the presence of Yetta. Triumphant at last that "He did it! He wasn't a kid" (295), Davey laughs at Ida, at his friend Natie, at everyone. Echoing Philip's question, "What is love?" Davey is without the playfulness behind Philip's reflection that "a woman is nothing very important." The attempt to avoid pain, however, is the same. The newly initiated man prepares himself for the way of Sam Linck: "What is love? Davey said as he turned into Ripple Street. What is love? A load of crap" (296).

Fuchs next shifts his attention to Philip, who is aware that his feelings for Ruth are not going to weigh enough against their class differences. Successive glimpses of hate-filled marriages, Davey's "feel" of Ida, and Cohen's project to become sexually initiated through the Communist Shura are followed by Philip's decision to forego sex with Ruth (298). A worrier and nurturer like his mother, Philip has to do what is best for Ruth. Although his own perspective on his involvement is predictably limited, his capacity for tenderness pulls against, perhaps redeems, the wretchedness of all the rest of Fuchs's miniature society.

Chapter 17 is another such cycle, the effect of its scenic syntax being that of love gone awry. Anna's return to find her husband and Marge in bed is followed by a scene in which young Natie the Buller steals Davey's girl Yetta. The next three sequences show Philip's learning by mail that he is losing Ruth to her family's pressures, the tiresomeness of his affair with the affected and wedded Tessie, and again the soured affair between Sam Linck and Marge. In this section all the relationships are characterized by some form of betrayal of the heart; the violences of the business world are temporarily overshadowed by variations on the failure of love.

By Fuchs's excluding Philip from essential glimpses of domestic struggle, by his attention to Philip's limited perspective, and by the significant arrangement of scenes, he places Philip gently within his society as part of it. Philip, "burdened" by traditional values of love, kindness, and honesty, frames his questioning in the terms of an artist attracted to the possibility of an empirical methodology that would be more truthful than a "concocted ordering" of his society's experience. The disintegration of values in that society is rendered in strongly naturalistic tones. But Fuchs finally rejects naturalism, through the unproductiveness of its methodology for Philip, and by the novel's selective arrangement of mysteries, which includes a fantasy of God. The author's final gesture of dismissal of the notion of inexorability is his refusal to show Philip's fate at the novel's conclusion.

Homage to Blenholt

A more controlled design, influenced by his readings of Joyce's *Ulysses,* is apparent in Fuchs's second novel than in his first. *Homage to Blenholt* covers only one-and-a-half days, from early one summer morning to the next afternoon, in the lives of a smaller group of characters than in *Summer in Williamsburg.* More attentive to formal divisions than in the earlier work, Fuchs titles his twelve chapters. Most of the action takes place in one building, the tenement in Williamsburg where the main characters live.[1] Having made use of the tenement setting in his first novel to reject the conventions of three genres, the *bildungsroman,* the naturalistic novel, and the social tract, Fuchs this time directs his technique of balancing disparate elements toward using the Williamsburg environment to turn comic conventions on end. The concluding double marriage, for example, a common resolution in comedies, including Shakespeare's, in *Homage to Blenholt* signifies spiritual death rather than regeneration.[2] Historically in comedy, clearly recognized social patterns either function as a corrective or are in need of correction. Fuchs conveys neither of these positions.

In accord with the theory of comedy advanced by Henri Bergson and George Meredith, positing the reader's attitude of superiority over the characters, one laughs at the people in *Homage to Blenholt* rather than with them. To foster that response, Fuchs provides farcical elements, which Paul Frederick Michelson associates with movie slapstick.[3] These elements include dominant traits that serve as indexes to a character's nature, such as Max's bizarre gait. Although the novel's harsh tone may have been influenced by the dismal sales of Fuchs's first novel the year before, the least spared of his objects of mockery is the sensitive and creative young man, Max Balkan, who is trying to use his mind to generate some success out of poverty in America.

Fuchs complicates his tone in several ways. At the same time that he has Max cut a ridiculous figure, he works into his comedy the story of mutual tenderness silently communicated between Max and his father, Label Balkan, a connection that evokes the Bloom-Dedalus bond. And though the combination of Max's lofty view of himself with his pattern of failures helps cast him as the classic types of both braggart and schlemiel, his genuine social limitations earn him some measure of sympathy. While the lack of common sense in Max and his friends, Mendel Munves and Coblenz, is a target of Fuchs's humor, their yearning for value and color in their existence is rendered appreciable. Their pretensions do not invite deflation, because they are a means of spiritual survival. Nonetheless, their eccentricities make them too laughable to arouse much identification.

As in his first novel, Fuchs shifts his attention among several characters, in this instance three young men and a boy living in the same tenement, whose fates undergo essential changes within the course of the day-and-a-half. Once again Fuchs undercuts received notions: the theme of these contrapuntal changes is not the conspicuous miseries of defeat within a materialistic New World, but the more penetrating and original notion of the perils of attaining one's desires. When success comes, in the second novel, it is not benign. In *Homage to Blenholt* Fuchs uses naturalistic material to convey an absurdist vision.

Max, Munves, and Coblenz, in their midtwenties, and the young boy named Heshey all live in a gloomy five-story tenement on Ripple Street, where other characters drop in without regard for privacy—Max's girl friend Ruth, the cleaning woman Mrs. Wohl, and a ubiquitous elderly Pearl Peddler. The three young men do not have jobs and are regarded, with some basis, as crazy by their community, but Fuchs carefully differentiates among them in their eccentricities, Max being fearful while Coblenz is fearsome, and Munves mild and abstract. Max lives with his parents and unmarried sister Rita, who, with the relentless support of her mother, is frantic to marry before she is too old to be attractive. Until her marriage, she shares the bedroom with Mrs. Balkan while Max sleeps with his father on a day bed in the living room. Coblenz and Munves are orphans, the former apparently living on his luck at the races and the latter on seven dollars a week from his brother-in-law in Rochester. Heshey, restricted from the streets by his mother and cowed by the tenement bully in the yard, applies his ingenuity to recreation and survival on the hall stairs.

The tenement-dwellers in this novel feel powerless and invaded, as in fact they are; yet, unlike the similarly frustrated souls in *Low Company*, they possess compassion for one another. For example,

Max commiserates over Heshey's indignities, as Label Balkan does over his son's. Yet none of them is in a position to help another, until Coblenz wins a large amount of money at the novel's climax. And that help—the money that everyone wants—turns out to be hardly a blessing.

The central story of *Homage* deals with Max's resolve to honor the racketeer Blenholt, Commissioner of Sewers, by attending his funeral, despite the last-minute withdrawal of Coblenz and Munves from their promise to accompany him. Max, who had never met Blenholt, regards him as the modern Tamburlaine, a figure who has attained power and therefore significance—the quality that Max's pattern of humiliation keeps denying him. The delayed bits of exposition about the man named in the book's title enhance Max's ridiculousness. The reader discovers on page 33 that Max never knew him, on page 48 that he was Commissioner of Sewers, on page 53 what Max's purpose is in going to the funeral, and on page 55 that Blenholt was a racketeer, an underworld ruler in both senses. We eventually learn the extent of his power during his funeral, with its disrupted eulogies, and of his deadly weakness during the mobsters' conversation afterwards: the boss, a diabetic, had died at the hospital from eating candy. This last fact about his Tamburlaine Max never learns.

Their own preoccupations keep Max's friends from recalling their promise to honor Blenholt. Coblenz is wracked in particular by a toothache exacerbated by the noise of children skating on the floor above his apartment, and in general by his anxieties that his wastrel life dishonors his decent merchant parents. Munves is jubilant over uncovering a minute error in linguistic scholarship. Max, persuaded that participating in the rites over Blenholt will inspire him to success and power, takes Ruth along. But Ruth yearns instead to see Joan Crawford at the Miramar Theatre and runs off when Max's efforts at manliness during a dispute at the funeral get him knocked down and trampled on.

Meanwhile, Max's too familiar mortification promises to end, even reverse itself, when an invention of his appears to have been accepted. After three phone calls and an invitation for Max from Mr. Atwater (Mrs. Balkan hears his name as "Hot Water") of Onagonda Onion, rumor spreads beyond the tenement of Max's success at last in the singularly American miracle: instant wealth through inventiveness and luck. But regardless of the merit of his idea for bottled onion juice, as with his other ideas such as canned orange juice, it had never occurred to him to discover whether it was already in use. In his office Atwater thanks Max for his interest with a five-pound sack of Onagonda onions, a symbolic burden of tears with which Max returns to face his jeering tenement public.

There is no character in the second novel aglow with prosperity like *Summer*'s Papravel. Aside from the cartoonlike glimpse of Atwater, the corporation executive, the only successful person in *Homage* is the deceased Blenholt, who is corrupt like Papravel. The characters whom the reader comes to know are accustomed to poverty, insult, and failure. On this summer day their unaccustomed victories bring to their lives grave changes that are in tension with the book's comedy.

Max becomes aware during his short-lived glory as a tycoon that his dreams have been at the expense of his father, who has been supporting the family by pacing the neighborhood sidewalks as a sandwich-board clown advertising Madame Clara's beauty salon. "Ideals, Max thought, the surge for power and significance, to live life in its turmoil, its fervor and variety—those desires were expensive" (248). Envisioning himself at the end of his struggles, Max finds his magnanimity: he vows to relieve his father and make things up to Ruth. Although the power to do so through bottled onion juice fails to come to him, the awareness remains.

The crushing visit with Atwater is not what changes Max; that disappointment is simply greater in degree than those in the past because he had never seemed so close to success. The permanent change, ironically marked only by his grieving father, is the new responsibility for others that constitutes, in Label's words, the "death of youth," of Max's imaginings, of his hope to be significant. Max comes to think that "he had been a kid and a fool, and it was time he gave up. All those fine ideals—the desire for the heroic spirit and a dignity in life—they were impossible, good enough for youngsters idling in high school. . . . A grown man could not afford the luxury of piquant speculation . . . while someone else paid the cost" (292). Coblenz's innocent greeting, "What's going on here? A funeral?" in the final scene evokes both the ritual at which Max has paid homage alone, and the import of the death occurring at the moment: Max is in the process of trading in his fanciful aspirations for a regular income and giving in to claims on him "as he meant to give in all the rest of his life" (300). Only Max's father, recognizing "the clamorous demands of the world . . . for resignation and surrender," sees Max's real death in his new resolve to live for bread alone (302).

Munves, too, has his life altered within a single day, through two uses of his imagination, intellectual and sensual. Devoting his mental energies to his Talmud of Anglo-Saxon place names, Munves suddenly finds what he is certain is the true location of the ancient Sealwudu, which the academicians have wrongly placed in Essex. Eager to share his jubilation with Rita, he relaxes his guard against the marriage snare. With help from her that includes a dancing lesson, he imagines the physical warmth of married life, disregarding the example of the Balkan household across the hall.

Rita's "hard day" at work alongside Munves brings her success on this day precisely because he is so confident of the importance of his discovery. Unwittingly he puns on Mr. Balkan's wry refrain, "Nu [Well], Columbus," feeling like a "new Columbus." The next morning he is disquieted by Rita's possessiveness, the rituals of intimacy, the destruction of his privacy, and the peril to his scholarly satisfactions. "Sealwudu," he says, "I hate you, why did you have to come into my life?" (247). The actual world of consequences, from which his etymological preciosities have protected him, intrudes itself because he grows too pleased over one of them.

Munves had hoped to bring variety to his confined life; he is finally fatalistic about the nature of the change that does come to him. Rationalizing his discovery of sexual feelings along with Sealwudu, he commits himself to slicing his days away at the meat-cutting machine, an operation which somehow mesmerizes him as research had done until now.

For Coblenz, ironic triumph occurs in the form of a gambler's fantasy realized: he dreams of a winning horse's name, Latabelle, bets on it confidently against impossible odds, and "cleans up." With this improbability Fuchs risks a *deus ex machina* in order to dramatize more than one point. Coblenz walks in upon calamity in the Balkan apartment—nothing but a sack of onions to rescue them—and cannot resist the chance to play God. By giving Mrs. Balkan his winnings, he gains admiration as the decent son of working Jewish parents rather than a drunken "goyish" good-for-nothing. As Max has known all along, money does swiftly replace scorn with homage. The Balkans' spectacle of instantaneous change toward Coblenz from disgust to esteem represents exactly what Max had dreamed of for himself. Coblenz realizes at once, though, that his melodramatic gesture leaves him the penniless good-for-nothing he has loathed being until his lucky vision of Latabelle.

Heshey, too, enjoys a dubious triumph, in his case thanks to his wits. Applying his motto that brains are more important than strength, Heshey devises a scheme to trap the ruffian Chink in the dumbwaiter shaft and bombard him with wet garbage. The success of his plan earns him delight in revenge and the new respect of his mortal foe. But his conquest leads him to repudiate Goldie, the girl whose cooperation made the conquest possible, and to enter an alliance with a scoundrel. Had he not succeeded in his trick to terrorize his terrorist, Heshey would have remained a Max-like victim, frightened and filled with righteous and impotent anger. Instead, as he proposes, he will provide the brains and Chink the muscle; rehearsing to be Blenholts, they immediately begin to scheme mischief against the notion of fair play, which they know to be useless. The price to Heshey's conscience is expressed in his "pang" at taunting Goldie. Yet his scolding mother, as if in homage to his new role of brute rather than victim, becomes newly solicitous.

Only one character in *Homage to Blenholt* knows the perils of believing in success. Label Balkan, Max's father, functions in the novel as a chorus with two major refrains. The first is his plaintive comment on the anomalies of the American dream, "Nu, nu! Columbus! America! Nu, nu!" (200). The other refrain is a warning against presuming good fortune, a "keneinerherra," which may be translated as dread of gloating. Unable to affect any turn of events, Label Balkan spits in order to cancel the evil of such presumption.

While the senior Balkan does not change during the novel, Fuchs makes clear the magnitude of his decline from an exuberant world-traveling actor. That loss and his genuine love for Max strengthen him as witness to the novel's central change; painted with artificial tears, Balkan grieves at the decline of his son, who is abandoning the individuality of his imaginative adventures for the institutions of marriage and delicatessen. As an actor Label had played Tamburlaine. His desire, radically unlike the expectations of others who worry about Max, is that his son have the freedom to be a "ganev," the freedom that defines the mythical America and makes a criminal not only a hero but a commissioner as well. Unlike Max Hayman in *Summer in Williamsburg,* who cherishes integrity, Balkan honors the amoral play of imagination, which he sees as equally fragile.

Fuchs does not appear to be ambivalent about America in this novel. Acerbic references to America or Columbus occur throughout, both explicitly and through irony. In particular Fuchs assails three aspects of American culture. One of these is the power of popular culture, which he depicts through its claims on his characters. Images and similes of Hollywood are common: Max asks a question "like George Raft in a hard movie" (86); Coblenz slinks down the hall to vandalize the offending neighbor's doorbell, "like Bela Lugosi trailing Boris Karloff" (116). Max despairs that in a movie the actor who says, "I am going to Monte Carlo" is immediately on the train, while in real life Max would break his trunk, lose the key, stumble into mud, and forget his tickets (189). Heartened by Mr. Atwater's invitation he imagines himself as "M. Sheridan Burlington," drinking cocktails and planning a trip to South America in his seaplane, his "presence the very epitome of the elegant mannerisms of the moving picture rich" (218). Munves bites off the end of his first cigar "as he had seen it done in the movies" (272); Coblenz feels "like Adophe Menjou, in the rain," after his gift to the Balkans, "despised by all and yet a heart of gold" (299). Ruth learns from movie magazines about La Nuit Pour L'Amour perfume and "brassieres with points" (39).

The pervasiveness of popular culture is evident in the novel's opening passage, when Max's conventional fantasy of Ali Baba merges with the picture of a woman on a banner advertising the Orocono Oil Company (11). Both images, alike the stuff of reverie, are interrupted by the shout of "a real boy" selling newspapers. Though America at seven in the morning seems "delicious" to Max, his day will be filled with failures, and the reader, following him, soon discovers the survival function of both sorts of dreams, those of Ali Baba, Don Quixote, and Xerxes, and those of commercial glamor.

What the young men in the tenement want is an end to their powerlessness through the use of their imaginations, from Heshey's battle strategem to Coblenz's stuporous epiphany. The novel's third page introduces the tension between "humiliation" or "indignity" and "grandeur" and "significance" (13). Max seeks grandeur as a means to significance. Young men in any culture may have similar desires, but the novel points up the tantalizing American context of wealth and admiration supposedly available to anyone. Young women contemplate their own manner of social significance through controlling a household, but their imaginations too hunger for more theatrical fare: Rita dreams of joining the royalty of Hollywood through Major Bowes's talent show.

Another aspect of American culture that Fuchs deals with in *Homage to Blenholt* is the resistance, the balking,[4] of the Balkan men against tedious employment in an industrialized society which they regard as murderous to the spirit. Sickened by such ungratifying work as pushing a handtruck twelve hours a day in the garment district, both dream about dignity, one in the past, the other in the future. Mr. Balkan manages to salvage theatricality by striking amusing poses for children in the street. He describes two kinds of work: honest, which is bad, like pressing or cutting all day, and "ganevish" (thievish), which is good, and includes the work of "gamblers, actors, poets, artists" (231–32). Though all these schemers—and one must suppose novelists are included—need luck, their chance to succeed lies in their inventiveness. "Honest" work is bad because it renders invention worthless.

The third element of American culture that comes under Fuchs's scrutiny is the popular definition of a man, that is to say, a successful man. The character Coblenz mocks this definition. The "true stature of man," he says, is measured by Caesar, Rockefeller, and Al Capone (295). From the point of view of Williamsburg, if not of Wall Street, it is hard to see the distinctions among these apparently diverse leaders. The implicit question dramatized throughout the novel is how Rockefeller and his kind can be very different from Capone and his sort. Coblenz, like Fuchs, has no faith in political reform to stanch the soul's ache; he calls communism just "a new happy ending" (297). But through these three related elements of American society—the power of popular culture, the imperiling of the imagination by ordinary livelihoods, and the measuring of manhood by wealth gained through any means—Fuchs conveys the falsity and waste of America's well-peddled dreams. The toll of success in a society with such standards is vividly realized when the bright and lonely child, Hesh, becomes a thug.

Despite the novel's astringent social comment, Fuchs's characterizations undercut facile themes. Though he shows capitalism taunting the poor while keeping them in place, he equivocates by casting Max as a schlemiel, a self-sabotaging loser. The complexity of Fuchs's treatment of Max Balkan is suggested in a parable Label Balkan tells about a dog in Kiev, one of the author's few instances of tropes. The dog in the story was confused by its mixed ancestry. He had sufficient parts of hunter to track and find his prey "and he knew it was asked from him he should get the animal. But he couldn't get it because the hunting dog in him, it wasn't strong enough or something. So he would yip and yip and cry like an angry baby . . ." (210). As Max suspects of himself, the dog had something essentially wrong with him.

Mr. Balkan intends to comfort Max with his passive thesis that happiness is the absence of pain and that effort brings pain: "Such an unhappy dog . . . , always torturing himself." But by the inherent insufficiency in the dog, the parable places cruelty not so much in society as in nature, or God, or the way things are. Although Max's ideas, like the one for paper toilet-seat covers, are both clever and practicable, and his mission to honor the king of the sewers has its charm, Fuchs does not portray him as a keen-minded idealist thwarted by a heartless social system.

Aside from being timid, foolhardy, clumsy, and overly dependent, Max is not, like Philip Hayman, an acute observer and a discriminating thinker. The reader comes to expect Max not to succeed. Though he yearns for importance, he is habituated to defeat, as we see in his ambiguous cry as he awakens on the morning of his appointment with Atwater: "He had unconsciously sent up a prayer to God not of joy but of fear, for pity and help," because "something might go wrong here as always" and "he might emerge only more ridiculous than ever" (228). This habit of defeat and his awareness of it are incongruous with his visions of being Caesar-like, and they distinguish him from his hero, Don Quixote, who never recognizes defeat during his adventures.

The opening paragraph of *Homage to Blenholt* discloses the contradictions of Max Balkan: between his noble self-conception and his "overlooking" of his limitedness. He is bound to earth with an "odd gait" (14) of which we are again reminded late in the novel (256).

> This was a peculiar [gait], involving a delaying, circular movement of the right hip which had the effect of kicking his right foot sharply forward in order to maintain the necessary rhythm. No man with such a mortal manner of walking had the right to think of himself as walking through unreality, but Balkan strode on, bathing deliciously in the tepid waters of his illusion, even though the repeated recurrences of that hip movement with its ensuing foot-kick resembled, spiritually, at least, the constant snifflings of a nose-cold sufferer. (P. 11)

One of Mrs. Balkan's kinder names for her husband is Chaplin. Max, like his father endearingly harmless, sets off on his day's journey resembling Chaplin's sweet little man as he "breathes a blessing" on the milkman's white horse. And his doom is as certain as that of Sisyphus.

The author's distance from this protagonist is quickly evident. Philip Hayman reads *Pendennis*, but Max Balkan is thinking about being Caesar, Xerxes, or Tamburlaine. The narrator refers to "the confused laboratory of his mind." Max advises Coblenz to confront his toothache by "investigating" his pain "with scientific detachment" (23), echoing Miller's advice in *Summer in Williamsburg*, which Philip follows. But Max is less like Philip than he is like Philip's friend Cohen, a source of humor in his emotional excesses.

Meeting Ruth in his front room as he runs in carrying his trousers, he cries out in great anguish and thinks, "Awkward, awkward! Always whenever he wanted to make an impression on a girl he had to do something to bust everything up. If Greta Garbo herself walked in on him one day he'd probably discover that his fly was open or something" (65).

Max's motif, like that of Cohen and of Shorty in *Low Company,* is humiliation: "No matter what he tried to do he always ended somehow in a drop from grace" (18). "Ridicule [overcame] him in a steady downpour" (30). "How unjust the world was!" (52), in its causing him to meet with "repeated failure and indignity" (60). Max's objections in themselves are worthy: "reality doesn't have to be dingy," he exclaims on seeing Blenholt's extravagant funeral (155). But characteristically "unvexed by reality" (13), he translates that observation to a celebration of extortion and vandalism. Whenever the portrayal of Max threatens to appear a polemic on behalf of misunderstood young writers (75), or of young men cornered by institutions like marriage (77), Fuchs makes him whine and overstate; the narrator notices when Max is "wallowing in disgust and self-pity" (78). Like Shubunka in *Low Company,* Max is led by his self-pity to what the narrator calls a "perverse" inventory of his abuses (207, 210, 211). Unlike Shubunka, Max has no idea that he is doing this.

The "confused laboratory" of [Max's] mind" interprets the worship of wealth as a form of idealism, so that he fails to notice the distinctions between two of his heroes, Caesar and Rockefeller, and another, Don Quixote. Max is like none of these, in fact, least of all Caesar. He never does what Heshey in this novel and the characters in *Low Company* do—become cruel in order to survive; he eschews brutality against others as well as against himself. But Fuchs makes his failure of vision about himself ridiculous.

The reader can sympathize with Max when Ruth misunderstands his citation from H. L. Mencken: "In such a country as this, with practically all human values reckoned in terms of dollars and cents, it is not only hopeless for a man to try to get on without money, but also a trifle absurd." Ruth interprets this passage as saying, "It's crazy for anybody not to get a job" (53–54). Max grasps what she misses, Mencken's objection to reckoning human values in dollars and cents. But money would be the means and measure of Max's power. Though he thinks and utters platitudes about "heroism, great feeling, high poetry, and a keen spirit of living" (54), his notion of the hero as absolute tyrant-extortionist makes him comical: his idealism is simply hunger for power. "Nobility! It was possible only

when you had power. A human being without money and influence
became ridiculous if he possessed only dignity instead" (183).
Aside from the humor in its being spoken by one so undignified,
this statement demonstrates how Max differs from Philip Hayman,
who admires the dignity he sees in his father.

Munves and Coblenz are similarly portrayed with ambivalence.
Munves is unworldly and unfocused: he claims to know "ten,
fifteen, twenty languages" and their dialects (50), and to be a member of the National Spelling Reform Society 147; he is lost in trivia.
Munves's delight, as the novel concludes, at the prospect of running
a delicatessen might be implausible, were it not for the motive
behind his scholarliness, which is to "keep a distance from the
mob" (95), the society of men that he wants to be part of. Munves
repeatedly passes the cigar store frequented by gentile taxi drivers
who physically harrass him and call him "Pishteppel," the Yiddish
word for chamberpot. While he condemns them as hoodlums, low
society, and a low crew (94), he yearns, like Heshey, to be chummy
with the "hard-boiled gentry whom he admired so much" (294), in
his view real men. When Coblenz arrives at the Balkan flat Munves
asks after the "boys," against whom his pedantry and isolation
have been his bastion. His plan at the end of the story is not only to
slice meat, but to make his delicatessen a place for people to
socialize.

One of Fuchs's brothers was a sometime linguist, like Munves.
Another was an inventor, like Max, though more successful in
selling patents.[5] Fuchs himself, like Coblenz, enjoyed betting on
horses, an irregular pastime for decent Jewish youths. Coblenz is at
first a wild, menacing drunk whose woes are comically treated
("Why me all the time? Why me?") but he grows more complicated
and is the most discerning of the novel's characters. Displaying an
awareness that is missing in Max, he thinks that attending
Blenholt's funeral is "a hot joke to do homage to a politician, a
gangster and a racketeer" (113). Coblenz is a cynic with a warm
heart, who plans a great bitter work of literature called "Epitaphs
and Epitaphs," possibly a parody of the diary of Fitzgerald's Jimmy
Gatz.

Chapter   I: Life's a Bowl of Cherries—All Rotten.

Chapter   II: Ninety-Nine Out of a Hundred People Are
              Lice. . . .

Chapter III: Go Fight City Hall.

Chapter IV: Fellow Passengers—To The Grave.

Chapter   V: Any Guy Who Works For a Living Is a Nut.

Chapter VI: Heroism Stinks Out Loud.

Chapter VII: Latabelle [the winning horse in his dream], I Love
       You. . . . (P. 112)

Though Coblenz insists that he believes in nothing but chance, he is
troubled that the goyish life he leads has "no meaning, no spirit, no
morale" (258). When he learns that his friend Max has "got himself
kicked in the pants again," Coblenz is moved.

> Now the apple barrel tenement of his soul rebelled and wept, a
> helpless boat rolling on the multitudinous seas of humankind's cruelty.
> Oh, the oompah, oompah, oompah of the soul. Couldn't you hear it
> crying like trumpets blowing over fields of daffodils? Couldn't you see
> it like a ship sailing the endless seas of Arctic gloom? Ta-ran-ta-ra!
> Ta-ran-ta-ra! The poor little dope, when would he ever get on to
> himself? (P. 295)

Possessing the greatest energy in the novel, Coblenz comes to
dominate it as he emerges from lunacy to credibility. By the conclusion he has become considerably more interesting than Max,
who has had the vitality squeezed out of him.

Women as well are characterized with mixed sympathies.
Heshey's abandonment of Goldie as being unworthy of his friendship reflects a social system unfair to females, yet at the same time
Fuchs makes it clear that Goldie is rehearsing to display the objec-
tionable traits of Williamsburg's adult women, when she derides
Heshey with "Sissy! Playing with girls!" Rita and Ruth are as
confined in their options as the men are; with their only hope the
doubtful blessing of marriage, the condition for young women like
these is war ("she didn't have to give up so easily," 148), a desperate
war to win "a fine bargain." Mrs. Balkan's unanticipated bargain
has been to bring up her children and run a business while her
husband was touring the world, only to see her earnings depleted
when he returned.

Mrs. Balkan is the most shrilly portrayed character in the novel.
Fuchs uses the word "savage" several times and the word "mali-
cious" to describe her; her most frequent tone he calls "high
derision." Yet her reveries of the old country thirty years ago
contribute to the novel's portrayal of conflict between the American
dream and harsh tenement life. Like some other notably overbear-

ing mothers in American literature, including Clifford Odets's Bessie Berger in *Awake and Sing!* and Tennessee Williams's Amanda Wingfield in *The Glass Menagerie,* Crenya Balkan gets her final-act opportunity for self-justification. She dreams of flowers in the countryside in Europe; she had worked hard in the grocery store she ran alone, but the money is gone; she has never ventured as far from the tenement as Macy's; she is fearful for her children; her ineffectual husband lives in abstraction. Insufferably goading to the end, Mrs. Balkan gains dimension from her narrow and disappointing history.

Ruth, like Mrs. Balkan, is introduced as vulgar and intrusive; she demands to read Max's mail and then berates him for what it contains: yet another disappointing reply about his inventions. Fuchs does not seem kind to her; "the woes of a nation upon her brow" (37) has the flavor of Nathanael West's reference to a shyster lawyer in *Miss Lonelyhearts* as "a son of the chosen." A campaigner like the other women in the story, she is bent on reshaping Max, whose thinking, like that of the Mencken whom he cites, is opaque to her. Max's romantic dreams are Ruth's enemy. Defining manhood as conformity, she presses him to be more "normal," in the belief that, unlike him, she accepts Williamsburg as it is. But Ruth is adrift in unreality as well, her primary fantasy being what she will create out of Max. Her compulsion to see the movie playing at the Miramar matches the intensity of his to attend Blenholt's funeral. Joan Crawford is Ruth's Tamburlaine.

Fuchs transforms Ruth's visit to the hairdresser (36 ff.) into a tour-de-force montage that connects images of Hollywood stars, confession tabloids, gossip columns, radio romance, and exotic beauty aids, all within the framework of a ritual that celebrates the social importance of a woman's appearance. Ruth believes that her hairdresser Marty, who earns forty dollars a week purveying these images along with the service of intimate banter and Adoration Shampoo, is a "regular man" in comparison with Max. Behaving as if her hair is all she has, Ruth is forever touching it and worrying about it. She has it fixed in a grotesque manner that is fashionable at the time, "plastered like corrugated cardboard." When she comforts Max, she strokes his hair as if his identity too were contained there.

The fact is that Ruth has little else to husband. Though Max appears to be dependent on her, she depends completely on his decision to marry her. Her connection to him is comically treated— she had given him "everything" by allowing him to hold her right breast for an hour, and so it was "too late!" for them not to spend their lives together. Yet it is clear that she believes she has no choice other than to wait for this "crazy" man to take her as partner. "Whadda dope! Whadda dope!" she thinks of him while her hair is drying. "He was hopeless, but what could she do?" (44).

In the course of the novel Ruth is embarrassed into a minor but noteworthy change in her perception of Max and herself.

> Max was a poet, a daydreamer, romantic, and she, who was destined to suffer much, was laboring to make his way an easy one in a hard, material world. She saw Max a success in her vision, walking down Fifth Avenue in striped trousers and with a cane, his expression sure and capable, a little gray running over the ears. She saw rotogravure pictures of Max and herself on the beaches of the Mediterranean Sea. Mr. and Mrs. Max Balkan, et cetera, and people at home, reading the Sunday papers, were saying: "She made a man of him. They all say he would be a nobody today if it wasn't for his wife."
>
> Ruth rose and blinked her eyes to wake up. "I'm getting just as crazy as him," she mumbled. (Pp. 172–73)

After this recognition of her own lapse in practical sense, Ruth becomes less hostile and more protective toward Max. Although she never essentially changes, Ruth is finally among those characters who attain some questionable victory: she wins Max.

Max's sister Rita grows ever more ugly in her sarcasm while she dreams of Major Bowes and Hollywood. She longs as her brother does to live not just safely and comfortably but as "kings and emperors" (42). If in America "all things were possible," Rita contemplates, then one could aspire to the farthest reaches of power. But weighted against such extravagant conjectures is the portrayal of her genuine desperation, and the revelation that she is not really deluded:

> I'll sit right down here this minute and pray to God for luck, Rita thought. All I need in the world is to know where Sealwudu belongs and when I find out, the Statue of Liberty will get so excited with joy, she'll fall down and drown. Munves gave her a pain. . . . Well, said Rita for solace, look at Ruth. She's got to run around with Max, and he's even crazier, and a fine bargain she'll get in the end. (P. 147)

Rita's plight is most sharply drawn as Fuchs juxtaposes a reverie of hers with a reminder of her true situation. She is imagining herself a "clamorous success" on the Major Bowes program, with offers from Metro-Goldwyn-Mayer and Paramount. In her vision she is "leaning over a bower of posies like Grace Moore, and singing: 'Love, your magic spell is everywhere.'"

78   WORLD WITHOUT HEROES

" 'Look,' cried Munves, holding up the middle finger [sic] of his right hand. 'A callus!'

" 'A callus!' exclaimed Rita. 'Let me see.' " (136) This descent from glory is consistent with the motif of falling experienced by the men characters in the novel.

While Fuchs writes with few apparent symbols, the "butterfly in the subway" being the one critics have noted, he does use a symbol in *Homage* which underscores his ambivalent tone. The motif of falling serves both farcically and seriously. Max's being knocked down on the hallway steps (35) is an objective correlative to his humiliation, and because of its timing parallels Heshey's defeat by Goldie. On the next page Max falls again and nearly has his glasses smashed. His most critical fall, though, is at Blenholt's funeral, when he is trampled on like a lowly object in "an angry swirl" and this time loses his glasses. "People kept digging their heels into all parts of his back, kept falling down on him with force every time he tried to raise himself to stand up" (169). What follows is a Walpurgisnacht of debasement reminiscent of Bloom's in Nighttown. He experiences his trip home "as though he was remaining stationary and Williamsburg instead was moving before him like a procession," with a montage of its sights, sounds, and smells.

Munves's variation on the motif of falling provides the comic incongruity of the pratfall by the pompous when, colliding with Heshey in the hallway, he is knocked off his feet (93), and when he later nearly falls while he imagines "nations [trembling] when he frowned. Emperors [would run] to do him honor," on account of Sealwudu (135). "For ten seconds he groped in the air madly, tried to grip the underside of the table with his knees, opened his mouth to gasp with the fear of crashing to the floor." In the first instance Rita picks him up, and in the second she saves him again: "But Rita was quick and straightened him out. The chair banged on all four legs again," as if to accentuate her practical influence. The third friend Coblenz does not fall but, a more aggressive soul than the others, announces he has thought of jumping from the roof (299).

The obverse of falling, rising, is associated in the novel with "the finish of all humiliation and petty abuse!" (251). Max confidently describes the Onagonda onion contract as "the first step on the ladder," his "first king [having] been conquered" (256). Both rising and falling figure playfully in the dumbwaiter episode, which begins when Goldie announces that Chink is "riding up and down for a good time" (186). Heshey's gain of Chink's amity is expressed by the narrative voice in terms that fleetingly apply as well to Max, Coblenz, and the two brides-to-be: "In one day he [Heshey] had managed to rise from the lowly" (280). In one day money enables Coblenz to ascend from disreputableness to godhead (298). He is able to transform abuse to adulation and manipulate people's destinies. His new power and Heshey's are ways to explore what may happen when one manages to achieve the long-elusive rise.

Through broader comic devices and a narrower scope than in his first novel, Fuchs dramatizes some of the same problems, particularly the yearnings of the spirit within a tenement environment and the drudgeries of making a living. But in *Homage to Blenholt*, his technique of comic exaggeration is a means of speculating on the effects of success, the object of desire, within the Williamsburg community. Though the plot is more ostensibly resolved than in *Summer in Williamsburg*, the apparent choices that the characters in the second novel make to bring about that resolution are joyless compromises—in Label Balkan's view of his son's fate, an unspeakable sacrifice.

Fuchs's use of comedy produces here a different tone for the same ambivalent vision in his first novel. By adapting the comic tradition of the double wedding to convey the death of youthful dreams, he demonstrates the malign power of social and economic forces. The absence, too, even the ridiculing of a hero figure is compatible with a naturalistic view. But by depicting protagonists who are absurdly maladroit, he invites the reader not to take seriously their spiritual deaths. Placing more attention on their foibles than on the forces that shaped them, he makes them appear as much victims of themselves as of anything else.

The conservative aspect of comedy is not to be found in *Homage to Blenholt*, that aspect by which social conventions are justified at the expense of the "different" personality, and which helps redefine and affirm what is normal. Fuchs is not truly revolutionary, either, in his mockery of what society makes acceptable, because, despite his criticism of American culture pointedly conveyed in such passages as the beauty-salon montage and Blenholt's remarkable funeral, he offers no alternative. He observes human failure with an attitude that invokes neither the cosmic moral order of tragedy nor the rational social order of traditional comedy. Fuchs implies the impossibility of change. And he approaches that condition with a clear-headed fusion of mockery and compassion.

6

Low Company

From time to time in the *Iliad,* Homer increases his range to portray mourners in opposing battlecamps who are grieving in identical rituals and preparing to inflict the same grief on someone else at daybreak. In *Low Company* Fuchs's characters behave with that failure of imagination which spawns cruelty. Only on rare occasions, a sympathetic connection is struck that enables one character to say, as does the narrator in a James Baldwin story, "My trouble made his real."[1] As Fuchs's characters perceive themselves abused by the hardness of others and by misfortune in general, their sense of injury deadens rather than quickens their fellow feeling. While the unacknowledged interdependence of these injured injurers is the notion that governs both plot and characterization, Fuchs demonstrates little hope that acknowledgement will occur. Had he denied all his characters an arrival at some awareness, his work would take on a necessitarian cast and therefore an ideology. By depicting one character to be capable of such an advance, Fuchs rescues his world picture from mechanical determinism. At the same time, by diminishing that single epiphany in relation to the novel's other events, he also avoids an optimistic ideology.

In *Low Company.* as in his other novels, Fuchs choreographs shifting perspectives as a stylistic analogue for the indeterminacy of values. Yet he keeps attention on the primacy of the value of fellow feeling through the destructive self-absorption of his circle of characters.

At the conclusion of Stephen Crane's story "The Blue Hotel" the Easterner tells the uncomprehending cowboy, "We are all in it! . . . Every sin is the result of a collaboration." The gambler who murdered the Swede, according to the Easterner, "came merely as a culmination, the apex of a human movement."[2] Like Crane, Fuchs isolates from a religious context the notion of communal responsibility that informs the structure of his work. Like Crane's story, too, Fuchs's novel concludes with conflicting patterns of resolution, sanguine in the education of one character, and yet pessimistic on the whole. Fuchs sustains this tension between hope and pessimism by various techniques of indeterminacy.

Low Company opens with its only explicitly religious passage, an excerpt from the Jewish prayer said on the eve of the Day of Atonement. The four chapters of the novel correspond to the recitation of the prayer four times during the Yom Kippur observance.

> We have trespassed, we have been faithless, we have robbed, we have spoken basely, we have committed iniquity, we have wrought unrighteousness, we have been presumptuous, we have done violence, we have forged lies, we have counselled evil, we have spoken falsely, we have scoffed, we have revolted, we have blasphemed, we have been rebellious, we have acted perversely, we have transgressed, we have persecuted, we have been stiff-necked, we have done wickedly, we have corrupted ourselves, we have committed abomination, we have gone astray, and we have led astray.
>
> O Lord our God, forgive us for the sin we have committed in hardening of the heart.

The editor of the authoritative Conservative Jewish prayerbooks, Rabbi Morris Silverman, explains that "it is characteristic of the spirit of Judaism that the confessional is recited in public and is expressed in the plural. Each human being is responsible for all the sins of the society in which he lives, either by his own acts of commission or by his passive acquiescence in the conditions that breed crime and lawlessness."[3] Fuchs's epigraph prepares for his uses of a microcosmic community as protagonist.

Despite such a prayer as its introduction, the context of *Low Company* anomalously diverges from that of the first two novels in not being identified as Jewish. While the actual Brighton Beach of the period was a melting-pot town with a large Jewish population, Fuchs leaves out specific indications of either Jewish, Italian, Irish, or other cultural components. In a solitary identification, Filipinos are referred to as owning amusement-park concessions. The only direct reference to Judaism besides the epigraph is a minor one in which Spitzbergen uses "them" as an example:

> "Nobody does what's good for them. Take the Jews. When they were slaves in Egypt, Moses came to them and begged to take them out but they didn't want to go. Ah," he sighed regretfully, "it's the same in every line." (P. 153)

Yiddish expressions in *Low Company* are few. Whereas common exclamations in the other novels were "oi, vay" or "Gevalt," here they are "Holy Smoke," "Gee whiz," "Jesus Christ," and for Karty, "Balls." No one reads *Der Tag* or calls another "schlemiel." Nor does Fuchs imply a Jewish society. While some of the characters, particularly the Spitzbergens, use Yiddish speech patterns, many do not: the soda jerker Shorty uses the Irish-American oath "B'gee" and ends many sentences with the refrain "don't you know?" Shubunka listens to a vaguely Christian theologian speaking on the radio who describes wickedness in terms of devils and Satans.

Another departure in Fuchs's third novel is his turning away from the traditional family and its symbols. Foremost among these is the dinner table, which is replaced by the counter and booths of an ice-cream parlor called "Ann's." The ice-cream parlor rather than the tenement flat serves as emotional hub for the circle of characters, who become a parodic family in their interdependence. The shop is in the resort community of Neptune Beach, the author's rendition of Brighton Beach, a section of Coney Island where he taught school for six years. Ann's is an ironic surrogate home, with its green-red-and-yellow walls and lights and futuristic table tops of Chromo Art-Metal; its pulsing heart is the cash register.

Most of the novel's action, even when it does not take place there, relates to the ice-cream parlor. When the young man Arthur keeps wanting to go "home" from the racetrack, he is referring to Ann's (175–76), not his boardinghouse room. Although his return may result in arrest, he longs to be back in the shop's warmth (259). Business deals and poker games are arranged at the soda shop; customers and employees turn to it for medical treatment and companionship as well as food; insults are exchanged familiarly; the gambler Karty virtually lives in the basement; the owner Spitzbergen, who has money and a fine home, stays until two every morning and returns on the subway before the breakfast customers arrive.

The Spitzbergens, Ann and Louis, are the ghost of a traditional central family, distantly removed from the Haymans and the Balkans. Ann has two identities: a beautiful and sadly idle woman who dines alone in a home that the reader never glimpses, and a gaudy shop named for her that functions as the nest for all the other characters. Louis, wed more to Ann's second aspect than her first, is both fussing hen and tyrant; all the vitality in the family is his, and it is directed away from their home. Far from being the powerful mother of the other novels, and in keeping with the atmosphere of sterility in *Low Company,* Ann passes her days in medical examinations.

Removing his characters from the Williamsburg subculture with its strong emphasis on the family, Fuchs portrays instead a miniature cosmos, lost and angry people from diverse backgrounds aboard a figurative lifeboat or Ship of Fools, at sea in Neptune. In his twenty-seven years Fuchs had developed an acute ear for English spoken by Eastern European Jewish immigrants, yet he was sufficiently worldly to understand that Jews were not the only transgressors described in the epigraph prayer. Without forfeiting the particularity of colorful speech, he mutes cultural identity in order to broaden his portrayal of reciprocal inhumanity. If his effort was also to escape being typed as a Jewish novelist, it has been largely unsuccessful up to the present.

The epigraph prayer serves the novel thematically in at least two ways. Directly, its list of iniquities is an inventory of the characters' actions in the story, and its cry of repentance for hardheartedness is the source of the motif of hearts like stone that recurs throughout the novel (104, 127, 128, 130, 145, 178, 182, 288). Shubunka's reflections on his transgressions at one point, though they shortly evolve into a self-consoling spectacle, particularize the list in terms of the Neptune cosmos.

> He told himself he had no right to be spared for he, too, had been faithless and had spoken cruelly, had robbed and done evil, had lied and exploited and persecuted and crippled. He had committed all the sins, not heeding their significance, arrogant and presumptuous within himself. When Karty, the poor gambler, came to him for money, it had pleased his fancy to turn him aside, and now the fat man regretted bitterly that he could not find him, give him the money, make him happy. (P. 254)

The epigraph also has an indirect significance. While children play a prominent role in Fuchs's other novels, the only children in *Low Company* are "piping" members of crowds. Nonrealistically, all the couples in the circle are childless. This absence of signs of continuity into the future evokes a precise loss. In Jewish belief, children of the deceased are obliged to recite the Kaddish prayer. Practicing Jews are congratulated on the birth of a son for that reason. The absence of survivors to pray for one is a variant of hell.[4]

Another dimension of Neptune's state of blight is the enmity that exists between the community and nature. " 'Rotten weather,' [Spitzbergen] scowled at the clear beautiful day, and he decided to go over the morning receipts" (154). Pleasant weather jeopardizes business; business sustains the group. The second day of the novel begins sunny and a little cool, a refreshing climate for summertime in Brooklyn, and consequently not an occasion for crowds to take the half-hour subway ride seeking relief in Neptune. That day it is apparent to Spitzbergen that "God was no longer over America" (204–5). The only garden described in the novel is "a little dirty area alongside of the stoop" of a dingy house, where "a ring of clam shells surrounded the scraggy broken bush" (227). The mythical evocations of these related elements—barrenness and a wrong relationship with nature—give force to the novel as Fuchs's rendition of the Waste Land. At the human center of this Waste Land is malice both bred of distress and breeding it.

The appropriateness of Coney Island as an apocalyptic emblem had already been discovered and widely used by graphic artists by the thirties. "Whether realists or modernists, they turned to Coney Island [for its] amusement complex scenes which were stunningly technological, urban, populous, egalitarian, erotic, hedonistic, dynamic, and culturally diverse."[5]

> Between 1910 and 1940 artists sought . . . to pinpoint the symbol as well as the fact of Coney Island. To [them it] was a mirror that showed key socio-political problems facing a fast-changing America. Coney Island as a microcosm of frenetic, machine-age New York City was their theme.
>
> These artists were not the only ones drawn to Coney Island. Over the years many onlookers spoke for or against this "American Babylon." Poets praised its romance, preachers assailed it as a "Sodom-by-the-Sea."[6]

To the artist Art Young in particular, at Coney Island "all the worst instincts of man and debilitating aspects of urban life came together in a frenzied, dehumanized setting."[7] During the twenties, for critic Bruce Bliven in *The New Republic,* "Coney held up a mirror to the larger society—albeit the grotesque distorting mirror of a fun house—and reflected a general crisis in American culture."[8] The crisis lay, according to Bliven, in the exploitation of the need for play within an urban, industrial setting. The irony of Coney Island as playground was that it was even more crowded than the setting left behind by the fleeing throngs. One writer recalls, "For me, in general, Coney Island was a littered, tawdry wasteland and the scene of endless childhood miseries. As a small child I never failed to get lost on the beach there. . . . I would suddenly find myself wandering amidst bewildering hordes of similar blankets and masses of humanity indistinguishable from one another in their near-nakedness."9

The dehumanization observed by critics of Coney Island was twofold. Affected by the rise of advertising as a social force, the amusement center naturally epitomized consumer values. But it also intensified the chief ills of the city—anonymity and its concomitant loss of social restraints. The authors of *Sodom By the Sea: An Affectionate History of Coney Island* tell not only of the crime, but also of the ballyhoo, freak shows, rigged game stands, police protection, bought politicians, and throngs of all the ethnic groups seeking entertainment. "To understand the crowd," French Premier Edouard Herriot declared after a visit in 1924, "one must go to Coney Island. The inexhaustible human river flows along the streets. . . . One is carried along into the torrent with all the languages and all the races of the globe . . . [in this] city of cheap pleasure."10

Fuchs chooses to focus on the amusement center late in the novel when Shubunka flees " in crazed panic" from the men who want to murder him. He arrives at the boardwalk so late that it is desolate though still brilliantly lit. The concessionaires "banged their counters monotonously with spoons, glaring hatred at the passersby because they would not stop. . . . The Ferris Wheel lumbered dispiritedly high above the ground, the cradles unoccupied. The weight-guessers, the health-talkers and the fortune-tellers sat moodily at their stands, unhappy with bad business" (269). Fuchs paints his desperate character into a setting which at its best moments is seamy, showing it graphically in its darkest aspect, like an image of the end of the world: Shubunka finds at the boardwalk amusement center not companionship and merriment but "only the bleakness of electric bulbs shining in dusty circles amid the emptiness."

Low Company contains many symbolic evocations in its beach-resort setting. The moral deterioration of its characters is echoed in the deterioration of Neptune by the forces of sand and sea.

> The sidewalks were broken in all those places where the blocks caved in. . . . Everything in Neptune Beach was sand. It was a misery. No matter how hard the street cleaners worked, shoveling the sand in mounds along the gutters, more blew in from the beach. On rainy days you walked in black gritty mud. Nothing was solid, neither the pavements nor the foundations of the buildings. (P. 28–29)

Though most of these descriptions are of Neptune's badly paved streets, the gradual collapse of the homes is symbolic as well.

Arthur notices during a poker game, for example, that the wall of Lurie's apartment is remarkably cracked. "It looks like a physical map of the United States," he says. " 'Neptune Beach,' confirmed Spitzbergen. 'All over Neptune' " (67).

Gabriel Miller has observed the parallels of *Low Company* with Eliot's *Waste Land,* advancing the idea of Spitzbergen ("peak of the mountain") as "a kind of debased fertility-god figure," whose sacrifice causes the sun to return.[11] Miller's comparison misses the essential disparities in vision between Eliot's poem and Fuchs's novel. Edmond L. Volpe, in "The Waste Land of Nathanael West," contrasts Eliot's hope with West's pessimism, in a passage that points up Fuchs's closer epistemological kinship with West.

> The land is arid [in Eliot's poem] because man's soul is arid. Since the Waste Land is man-made, it is within man's power to regenerate his dead world. . . . Eliot's Waste Land is not the product of forces beyond human control. There is supreme order in the universe. Man, individually, need only submit to God, the source of that order. By submitting, man can bring order into his own soul and thereby into his world."[12]

For both West and Fuchs, on the contrary, the physical world is undirected, and human beings cope with its disorder by their delusions about imposing order. Fertility rituals, in accord with the observed order of seasonal rhythms, celebrate a resurrection after winter's deathlike state, but the return to normal activity on the third morning that concludes *Low Company* is not a return to health. The death of the emotionally infirm fountain-king Spitzbergen does not produce fruitfulness. Rather, Ann's and Neptune Beach will flourish only to the degree that the sun scorches Brooklyn and drives consumers to purchase solace. The rain of life and the refreshing breeze are death to the ice-cream-parlor community, including the questing knight Lurie, who is a shopkeeper. Neptune Beach as whore has no way to right its relationship with nature.

Eliot's poem begins with Part 1, "The Burial of the Dead." Fuchs's novel begins with the prayer recited when the dead are remembered after their burial. Eliot's line express the same waste of mortality through solipsism that Fuchs's novel depicts: "We think of the key, each in his prison/Thinking of the key, each confirms a prison" (414–15). But while both works suggest that sympathy and a yielding spirit are life's only hope, Fuchs's tone is at the same time more sympathetic and less hopeful than Eliot's.

Despite the density and intricacy of the plot that James T. Farrell praised for its pacing, despite its weaving together of seven separate stories, *Low Company* is on one level a murder story. Fuchs creates suspense by several means, including the stalking of three characters, Shubunka, Karty, and Spitzbergen. The murder, rather than being committed by gangsters who cruise in large black sedans, is committed by one of these hunted figures, Karty, whose desperation and sense of injury are the most compelling in the group at Ann's.

The plot covers exactly three days. As in *Ulysses*, the marking of the passing hours on the clock intensifies suspense by signifying various hopes and dreads; yet unlike Joyce's novel and in keeping with its own surreal nature, *Low Company* contains no mention of the year, month, or days of the week. Only a reference during the poker game to Max Schmeling's defeat of Joe Louis places the time in late June of 1936 (67–68).

In the novel's four chapters, which resemble acts in a play divided into scenes and sub-scenes, the urgencies of various members of the group heighten hourly and are intricately related. The plot strands are seven: the efforts of the coward-braggart soda jerk Shorty to seduce a languid Russian widow, Madame Pavlovna; the crazed gambler Karty's struggles to appease his violent brothers-in-law, from whom he has stolen; the turn of events for Herbert Lurie, a dress-shop owner, about to marry a second time as a means of escaping from Neptune; the consequences for Arthur, an unworldly dishwasher, of borrowing from the cash register to help Karty; the Syndicate's death threat to Shubunka, a brothel-keeper whom it is ousting from dominance in the area; the entanglement of Spitzbergen, the stingy owner of Ann's and lessor of apartments for prostitution, who has to negotiate with the new crime boss in town; and the Syndicate's threats to the survival of the soda parlor itself.

The action advances through betrayals. Karty has stolen money from his wife's brothers before the story begins; Spitzbergen turns against his associate Shubunka after gangsters vandalize his shop; though both of them are wealthy men, Spitzbergen and Shubunka refuse money to the frantic Karty; Arthur takes money from the cash register; Karty strangles Spitzbergen for money and ruins Arthur's life by making him his accomplice. A comic betrayal occurs as well when Madame Pavlovna balks at Shorty's inelegant demands for sex after his investment in an evening out, and a benign betrayal occurs when Lurie, coming to recognize the delusions that have prompted him to want Dorothy, allows a confrontation over Shubunka to end their marriage plans.

The individual characters who are engaged in this network of betrayals are rendered with the balance of ridicule and understanding that infuses *Homage to Blenholt*. The humor in *Low Company,* which exists primarily in the episodes about Shorty, reflects that sustained gentle ambivalence. But the group, cursed by its separate members, cumulatively forms a character that Fuchs finds ugly in its stoneheartedness. I will discuss first the individual characters and then the group as they function in Fuchs's variation on the wasteland theme.

Herbert Lurie, owner of a local dress shop, is the single character whose reflective powers make his experiences in the course of the novel useful, as when "with a sinking rush of clearness he could envision what [life with Dorothy] would be" (302). Though he does not receive more attention than a half dozen other characters, he provides credible observations about conditions in Neptune and about his own development. The "boys" at Ann's are greedy and without sentiment, he tells us early (32), Neptune Beach is "concentrated wholly on desire and the process of its satisfaction, abject and mean" (179), and what he wants to escape is "the life in Neptune Beach [which] was poor and empty, mean, without beauty or aspiration" (301).

In his midthirties and divorced, Herbert has been living with a woman, Flo, while courting Dorothy, the cashier-waitress at Ann's. Herbert's problem with women has been that he expects them to transform the conditions of his life. Not only does his domestic record make his prospects appear cheerless, but Dorothy's concern for appearances is made repellent to the reader and grows increasingly so to Lurie. His hope thins on the eve of his wedding as he notices clues to the trap of Dorothy's loveless bargain as well as clues to his own ambivalence, like not being able to say "love" (239). As he comes to recognize with shame, "he was plunging into marriage recklessly, not because of the girl but from some impelling desire within himself. It was as though he thought a new wife would mean a new world for him and an end to the dingy, lifeless ways he knew. It was as though any new wife would do" (240–41).

Lurie's more substantial relationship in the novel is with Shubunka, because it transforms him and his other relationships. When he discovers what Shubunka's low business is and watches Shubunka suffer a beating, Lurie is impersonal and disgusted. "Shubunka's troubles were not his concern and there was nothing he could do anyhow" (182). When Lurie refuses his apartment as a hideout, Shubunka cries, "He wants to get married. All right. He don't want troubles. . . . What hurts another he don't care" (183). Lurie's sense of having failed the other man grows from that point until Shubunka's naked and lonely terror of the gunmen stalking him makes Lurie aware of his own stoniness. And when Shubunka, in that state of terror, shows real distress at having upset Dorothy, Lurie is profoundly moved. "He realized with a pang his own hardness in driving Shubunka into loneliness when the fat man needed warmth and aid. No one had good in his heart, not even he himself in spite of his innermost distaste for Neptune Beach and its calloused men" (238).

The novel's only positive advances toward consciousness are in these two figures. While Shubunka's new condition of awareness is finally inscrutable and hopeless—"He knew it was over" (311)—Lurie's growth is comprehensible, as, unlike Huck and George Willard, he "lights out" for his home. Pity fills Lurie, and "the mood of despondency which had oppressed him all day . . . suddenly lifted." Shubunka's "complete wretchedness" and yet resignation to his fate make Lurie feel "clear and sure."

> Lurie knew now that it had been insensible and inhuman for him, too, simply to hate Neptune and seek escape from it. This also was hard and ignorant, lacking human compassion. He had known the people at Ann's in their lowness and had been repelled by them, but now it seemed to him that he understood how their evil appeared in their impoverished dingy lives and, further, how miserable their own evil rendered them. It was not enough to call them low and pass on. (P. 311)

Lurie's response is prevented from being sentimental by his suspicions of Shubunka's posturing as a means to manipulate and involve him (183), and by his honesty with himself about having wanted to escape from Neptune through Dorothy. Whereas most of the characters in the novel express fear of the cost of getting involved in what is not their business, Lurie alone finally gains by losing his stoniness, the hard heart of the epigraph.

Shorty, who uses his name Thomas only once, to sign a love letter (160), is a lonely bachelor over forty whose protestations betray him: "I don't want to go around making an impression," he says, but this is his obsession. A braggart about spurious conquests, Shorty "can't stand them guys who are always shooting off their mouths about the broads they got" (27). According to his "sense of honor," "Kiss and tell, that's no way for a regular guy" (191), but he boasts to the new cashier that Madame Pavlovna longs for him. Shorty's point of pride among the men, including his barber, is that "when I feel the inclination, I don't have to pay for it!" (193), but in fact his excitement about Sophia Pavlovna's encouragement springs from not having, for once, to visit a prostitute. During their date, nevertheless, he tallies his expenses for the "normal and free" access to her favors. In keeping with Fuchs's attention to the commercial element in legitimized dealings between men and women—marriage is a business, as Dorothy's parents make clear—Shorty is righteously indignant when Sophia's response is not commensurate with his investment.

Alternately obsequious and blustery, Shorty displays most farcically the group's hypocrisies. "Vicious with his private despair" (69), he regards himself as persecuted and too generous to survive (161). He defines masculinity by movie images: exhaling grandly like Ronald Coleman (26), threatening to beat up hoodlums in the manner of James Cagney (44), and preparing his Ronald Coleman expression as he waits for Madame Pavlovna on her sofa (244). Partly through their comically childish exchange of letters, Fuchs makes what happens between the soda jerk and the corsetiere somehow matter. After being tossed out of Sophia's parlor, Shorty despairs of a world in which there is no moral reason, "no cause and effect" (274), one in which someone as good as he can be treated so unfairly (281).

Sophia Pavlovna, who owns a corset shop next door, has been coming in each morning for three months for a regular breakfast and a few discreet words with "Shurtee." Sophia lives on musty picture albums and laments never having had children. Smiling a "blissful, distant smile" (139) she combines pretensions of refinement with nostalgia about travel to Nice, Bombay, the Persian desert, and "Hahvahnah," with her husband, who sold women's underwear. Sophia alone utters, once, the novel's key theme: "You have no charity," she admonishes Shorty (140). Uncertain in her romantic vagueness about what to do with the odd little man, she flirts and giggles until his crudeness provokes her to lift him and throw him out. She pronounces him "Cockroach" and leaves him to seek assuagement for his humiliation; he does so by harassing the new cashier, Lillian, and cornering her in the sodashop basement.

Arthur, the dishwasher at Ann's, is a bewildered innocent far from his home in Springfield, Massachusetts, where he drove a delivery truck until three weeks before. Along with Lurie and Shubunka, he is one of the three characters who are changed in the course of the three days, but his change is corrupting. Eager, respectful, and astonished by people's behavior, Arthur characteristically stares with his mouth open. His dreamy vulnerability is given emphasis through his hands (11), as he takes sensuous and aesthetic pleasure in playing at washing dishes. Reminiscing in the midst of a poker game about the smell of a boxthorne tree (68), Arthur is all credulous and is therefore eccentric in the group at Ann's.

Arthur's corruption is inevitable because of the contradiction between his two ambitions: unaware that he is as carefree as he will ever be, he longs to be "free as a bird, with nothing on his mind." He is at the same time curious to know things that will make him a man, as he defines one. Deception, like the risks of gambling, is to him a mark of manliness (48), and on learning of Shubunka's income from brothels, he is impressed that Shubunka is a real man (59). Lurie observes with sympathy the danger facing Arthur, but he is too filled with his own troubles to help. When Arthur is at Aqueduct the reference that a bettor makes to Chester Gillette, the model for Dreiser's Clyde Griffiths, sounds a warning for the reader but one that the young dishwasher would naturally miss:

> "Biggest thrill I ever had in my time was that day in Albany. Nineteen seven. Ever hear of Chester Gillette?"
>
> "Who? I don't know about race horses. See, I ain't familiar in that line."
>
> "They burned him in nineteen seven. The *American Tragedy* feller. Man wrote a book about him once. Well," he spoke with easy nonchalance for all of his importance, "I sat in the very same electric chair a couple of hours after they burned him. Yes, just for the hell of it."
>
> "You don't say!" gasped Arthur, "Really?" (Pp. 172–73)

"Free as a bird" grows in meaning from the time Arthur's only problems are boredom and inexperience to the scene on the train when he realizes that he has done something seriously wrong by allowing Karty to maneuver him into taking twenty dollars from the cash register (201). While generosity serves Lurie well, it is costly for Arthur, whose impulse to help Karty is uninformed, while Lurie's kindness to Shubunka is sifted through doubt and reflection.

Arthur's error is costly for Spitzbergen as well as for himself. Ann has extracted a promise from Louis that he would go home earlier than usual, and he intends to do so. At the scheduled time Karty is in the movie theater. The discovery of a cash-register theft detains Spitzbergen at the shop until after Karty leaves the Mermaid Theatre. The next day Karty would have been "put in the hospital" by his brothers-in-law, and Spitzbergen would have lived.

"Trotting" around with his mouth open, absently carving pictures in the soap suds, or blurting out an irrelevancy at a poker game, Arthur is portrayed with considerable tenderness. He is unique among the circle at Ann's in touching Karty's elbow comfortingly when he appreciates the gambler's anguish (261). But Arthur's innocence is not simple: though he becomes certain that Karty is waiting for Spitzbergen with a piece of iron in his pocket, Arthur continues to follow his frenzied companion, who draws courage from his presence. Arthur, habitually obedient, misses the opportunity to thwart Spitzbergen's murder by leaving Karty. He is indeed Karty's accomplice, his perverse innocence functioning destructively.

Louis Spitzbergen recognizes that he is a consummate miser but, like all the other aberrants in the story, he protests his helplessness. "It's my nature to be aggravated. I can't help it," he tells his wife as she tries to sooth him (202–3). The process of getting and not spending appears to be the focus rather than the source of his chronic exasperation. "Let me make a penny. It's coming to me, ain't it?" (207).

Spitzbergen, "mountainpeak," is called the "boss" more frequently as his death nears, and the plot is constructed so that his murder is at its climax. Spitzbergen's other preoccupation than money is his mortality, which is the keynote of his formulaic laments. His Yiddish idioms produce varieties of irony besides the foreshadowing of his murder. Early he avoids his wife's phone calls with "Tell her I just dropped dead," and such references grow more frequent as the time grows close: "As long as I live and be well, leave me my life" (264), "I'm still in the world yet" (267), and "better off dead" (267). These remarks also underscore the fact that Spitzbergen believes the gangsters are his menace (78), while it is in truth a familiar figure in the soda shop. Spitzbergen has the thugs in mind when he twice calls himself "a man standing under a knife" (127, 213).

Considerable dark comedy is produced through the enormity of this wealthy man's miserliness, his slogans being "I got to make a living" (216) and repeatedly "business is business." His obsession is the most literal variation on the lack of generosity the characters display. Spitzbergen is pleased by his wife as his lovely possession, but her expensive hypochondria adds to his worries. Although Ann's brief visit to her husband shows the comfort he finds "beneath her warm gaze" (157), the moment she leaves he returns to his participation in the wretched circle. After shouting abuses at the tearful new cashier Lillian and threatening her with prison—"You can cry your head off"—he bemoans his persecution by all the stinking world's agents. "Thieves, gangsters, rotten weather. Only miseries. He had a monopoly on them." And worst of all, he thinks, weeping shortly before his murder, "his days . . . would continue in the same fashion" (266–67).

All of Spitzbergen's energies are devoted to the shop, but he has other sources of income besides Ann's. His mortgages on tenements and ramshackle bungalows bring him into contact with Shubunka, who, as "booker," rents space from him and pays handsomely and promptly. Just as the soda man's credo that business is business rationalizes his tyranny and pennypinching at Ann's, his conviction that dealing with Shubunka is simply business helps Spitzbergen deny his complicity in creating his own recent troubles. His role in the cycle is made plain when the narrative voice observes his indifference to the possibility of Shubunka's murder. "Hearing the casual news that a fellow human might well be murdered, [Spitzbergen] felt intense sorrow for his own misery, and he bewailed the fact that he might never see Shubunka again or the two weeks rent money he owed him" (116). Treacherous to the booker in order to preserve his eighteen-thousand-dollar investment in the soda parlor, he hypocritically tells Shubunka of his concern for him: "Do you think my heart is a stone?" (127).

Moe Karty and his wife Bella are estranged by his racetrack addiction and his consuming bitterness at not having wealth and prestige. Karty has stolen thirteen hundred dollars from his wife's brothers while he worked as an accountant for their garage, and her protectiveness of him against them enrages him more than their vengefulness. Described throughout the book as weasellike, with a "nose like a snout," Karty is monomaniacal in substituting faith in luck for judgment (201). He grumbles in jargon about distribution of wealth; according to his ethic, Spitzbergen doesn't deserve to have money because he hoards it, and money was not intended to be stored in banks. But Karty's refusal to work (172) keeps his rant against the exploitative rich from being convincing. Moe Karty's wish is to have people running to him, wanting to know him, because of his wealth. In this respect he resembles Max in *Homage,* but Karty is more hostile and dangerous and less comically treated.

In fact, Karty is the most depraved of the group at Ann's, and for more than his ultimate murder of Spitzbergen. The epigraph prayer ends its list of iniquities with "we have led astray." Serious damage to Arthur's life results from Karty's corruption of him, yet Karty thinks only of the wrongs done to him by society in general and by those in Neptune who have failed to rescue him from the consequences of his gambling addiction.

Within the novel's context, depraved as he is, Karty is right about their failure, as Shubunka understands when his own misery reaches bottom and he tries to find Karty to give him money. When he had turned to Shubunka Karty's desperation was real, his tears were real, and the danger of his being maimed or killed by his creditors was real.

Shubunka, who has no other name,[13] is the most fully developed and unforgettable character in Fuchs's body of fiction. Shubunka has about him qualities that are either the stuff of legend or a mockery of it, or both. Richard Chase writes of McTeague that "we should have to change our feeling about him if his name were Joe McTeague, say, instead of apparently just plain McTeague."[14] But Shubunka signals quite different notions about social degeneration from those of Norris's Nietzschean blond beast.

Before Shubunka's first appearance, as late as page 55, he is the subject of accumulating introductory clues, in the mode of Molière's *Tartuffe,* who never appears in Act 1 but acquires force through references to him. Early remarks about the booker establish him as someone in authority—"Shubunka said it was all right" (7)—but before long he becomes associated with trouble. Though decidedly more complex than Papravel in the first novel, Shubunka too calls himself an honest businessman. His business is the management of forty prostitutes in eighteen houses. Over a period of eight years Shubunka has acquired sufficient wealth to earn the prestige that Shorty and Karty long for, but he grieves because his wealth is all that elicits people's deference. Missing family and friends, he contrives to enjoy a measure of companionship with the group at Ann's by organizing poker games.

Fuchs characterizes Shubunka with a Flaubertian balance of sympathies and antipathies as he locates him in the network of inhumaneness among the low company. The fact is that children still taunt Shubunka as King Kong (120), Dorothy rudely rebuffs his efforts to be gracious about her wedding, and the appearance of the fat whoremonger waddling on poorly healed broken legs is odious to women. At the same time, Shubunka is "nourished by the dramatic conception of himself" (120), finding "refuge [in] his self-dramatization" (121).

Lurie is disgusted by "the relish [Shubunka takes] in his mortification" (181), after two henchmen warn him to leave town. As the thugs start to leave, Shubunka creates a spectacle and provokes a beating by demanding that they accept his watch as a token of friendship. Like Max Balkan in his daydreams and Label Balkan in his clown-strutting, Shubunka creates a drama out of his humiliation, conscious of Lurie as his audience. Our experience of Shubunka's humiliation is undercut by his moral myopia: appealing on humanitarian grounds, the merchandiser of women reminds the thugs of how human beings should behave toward one another (151).

Before the evening when he is to confront mortal fear, Shubunka defines baseness as any unevenhanded dealing with him, for example, asking for money but not visiting when he is ill, or failing to "lift a finger on his behalf" (129). When Karty grovels before him for money (130), Shubunka's self-absorption about Spitzbergen's defection cancels his spontaneous humane response to Karty's situation. He tells Karty that he understands his danger, and he does, but he thinks, "I can help but where can I turn?" (129). This kind of self-absorption works reciprocally in various sets of relationships in the circle. An example of its great cost is the impact on Dorothy's life of the fat man she loathes: Shubunka's arrival at the new apartment permits her hatefulness toward him to crystallize Herbert's doubts about marrying her.

The major strength in Shubunka's characterization is the ambiguity created by his compulsion to dramatize anguish that is genuine. He does not even require an actual audience but can just as well imagine one:

> In that peculiarly lit room, with the distant murmur of the radio, Shubunka lay alone, feeling himself somehow noble and tragic. It seemed to him that the world must be watching him as an actor is viewed by his audience, with intense sympathy, with pity and concern, with avid apprehension at his inevitable downfall. Certainly this was the way he wanted it, and every movement, every thought in his head, the expression on his face, was conditioned by its conceived effect upon this invisible audience. Shubunka relished their pity and the tears, imaginary as they were, for he had no others to turn to. (P. 252)

When Shubunka confesses to Lurie that he is aware of being a moral monster (180–81), elaborating with "cases and instances" of his meanness, Lurie, disgusted, senses that Shubunka is "having a good time" through abjectness. But while Lurie is slow to think such a buffoon in earnest, he observes that being terrorized by the crime syndicate causes a serious change in Shubunka: "Now he seemed to be a man completely engrossed in fear so that no room was left for affectation" (303), and "in his great fear and misery Shubunka could now think of nothing but what he had done to Lurie and Dorothy" (307). "For the first time," Lurie comprehends the logic of the man, so that he regards further instances of apparent spectacle as simply part of the man and not to be judged (309). With Shubunka purged of self-pity as he simply fades towards some existence in Troy, New York (311), Fuchs finally removes that impediment to the reader's compassion.

Because Shubunka needs to hide from the gangsters only over-night, one may ask why Fuchs does not have him rent a room somewhere, or have Lurie rent one for him as he earlier proposes. Although Lurie's reasons may have to do with precipitating an end with Dorothy, Shubunka's reason is consistent with all of his be-havior—the lessening of aloneness. Lurie's apartment is more than simply a means of staving off Shubunka's murder; it makes possible a human connection. And Lurie's invitation, after Shubunka has said only "Please" to Dorothy, is finally more precious to the booker than living. The offer having been made, he does not stay at the apartment.

Shubunka is not killed but survives, utterly broken. Fuchs, true to his method of twisting conventions into incomplete resolutions, burlesques the obligatory killing-off of the defeated criminal at the end of gangster films. At the same time, Shubunka's effect on Lurie, Lurie's sense of Shubunka's experience, is the low company's re-deeming element and *Low Company*'s single note of hope. The tension in the novel between hope and no hope depends on the force of Lurie's realization as it weighs against the otherwise per-vasive grimness of Fuchs's fictional society.[15]

Like Shubunka, all the individual characters at Ann's, though they are depicted as distorted by their respective obsessions, are handled with a measure of tenderness that gives them dimension. In Fuchs's treatment of the wider circles, on the other hand, the larger the group being represented, the more acerbic the picture. Neptune Beach is grim and seedy, the crowds are ugly in their determination to have a good time (227). The word "garish" appears often, with supporting images. In the dark and cracked stucco houses,

> [t]he rooms were dark and empty but the radios had been turned on. A confusion of melodies, speeches and wisecracks raucously poured out into the street so that no single program was distinguishable. But no one seemed to mind, for no one really listened to the music or the speakers. It was as though they needed the metallic racket of the radios to serve as a base on top of which they might shout out their own conversations. (P. 227)

The faces of shop customers look "sick and distorted" (215). Sav-age onlookers take pleasure in Karty's beating by his wife's broth-ers, and customers at Ann's delight in Karty's outburst at Shubunka

(131). In both cases children are as bloodthirsty as adults. The three brothers of Bella Karty are an undifferentiated pack with "businesslike" faces (229), no better, perhaps worse, than the gangsters as they stalk Moe to cripple him in the interest of justice (235). Spectators at the Mermaid Theatre watch an argument "with keen relish" (220). When Shubunka is the target of shots, his annoyed neighbors disregard the possibility of a victim. Even the promisingly "intellectual" old man who interrupts Karty's beating with a pan of water vents his general rage by threatening with a second pan. The betting ring at Aqueduct is an inferno (175). In descriptions that anticipate the closing passages of West's *Day of the Locust,* Fuchs conveys the swirling impersonality of its mob (164, 174).

> The thousands of race-goers ran about, pushing their way, tripping and falling in their hurry. No one stood still. Each man was in constant action, going to a place near the rail, hopping in the air to look over people's heads for the horses, rushing back to companions from the betting ring or deciding on last-minute wagers and chasing back to the shed in a fury lest he be too late. To Arthur, sitting high in the stands, the crowd seemed to become a single unit, in constant motion but according to a definite pattern and design, like an ocean swell and fall. (P. 164–65)

This eddying mass has the force to catch Arthur up and carry him away from a good position in the betting ring to the grass outside (174).

The ugliness of the crowd, as the context in which the individuals at Ann's behave, tempers their failings. But while Fuchs presents that condition as a factor, he avoids the determinism that would make his characters less interesting. The result produced by this balance is the dramatization of the unresolved question of accountability. For example, the coarseness of Spitzbergen's customers and of their tastes mitigates his disagreeableness as he strains to please them for small amounts, ten and fifteen cents a sale. "Spitzbergen's ears cracked with the racket, his eyes were dazzled by the lights, but that was what his customers wanted at night, romance, bright colors and music. It was business and he supplied the radio and the lights without a murmur, even though the electric bills were enormous" (105). And Karty's "sure thing" madness is the habit of mind in thousands of bettors at the track, their passions served by an elaborate system.

Both the dramatic tightness and pacing of the plot, noted by Farrell, and the relationship between the smaller and the larger society are nowhere more evident than in the section where Karty takes Arthur to Aqueduct (163–77). Tension heightens through the reader's certainty that Karty will not be prudent enough to reserve twenty dollars to protect Arthur's job and freedom. In the Aqueduct sequence Fuchs moves his focus simultaneously in closer to Arthur and out to encompass the racetrack world; Arthur trusts his fate to the near-berserk Karty the way Karty and a mass of other bettors do to blind chance. Here, as in his other novels, Fuchs portrays characters at various stages in their degeneration into hardness. Arthur's loss of innocence, together with the particularizing of a few bettors in the stands, suggests that there has been such a turning point for each of the others in the crowd. Arthur's own crisis had been the earlier moment at the cash register, more tentative even than Hurstwood's at the safe in *Sister Carrie*. Despite Arthur's hatred for materialism (176), he is caught up by his eagerness to please in general, his kindly feelings for Karty, Karty's severe intimidation, and the young man's desire to join the men and live as he imagines they do.

The most telling association between the familiar circle and its wider contexts is represented in the nameless storekeepers of Neptune Beach, with whom Fuchs opens and closes the novel. As the story begins, they stand on their doorsteps observing the drizzling weather, and at its conclusion these replicas of Spitzbergen read of his murder. Stifling any inclination to mourn so that they may get ready for their customers, the merchants repeat Spitzbergen's deadly slogan: "business was business and a man had to make a living." On the third morning the sun blazes in the damp atmosphere to create a steamy and chafing blanket that will stimulate trade. There is still a God over America.

In his other novels Fuchs closes with scenes of familiar characters. In *Low Company* he makes his final sentence trenchant by using the storekeepers as a multiple mirroring of Spitzbergen, with the implication that all of the shops conceal grotesques with their own sagas. "Going inside the stores, they scratched their chins thoughtfully and said it was a pity the soda man wasn't alive to enjoy the wonderful weather" (314). Each withdraws to business, and Spitzbergen is not discussed.

This concluding line economically organizes a series of evocations that are central to Fuchs's portrayal of Neptune. "Stores" suggests the evil practices demonstrated to be necessary in the mercantile community of Spitzbergen, Shubunka, and Lurie. The word "thoughtfully" emphasizes that the worries of the marketplace occupy the merchants rather than genuine reflection after a fresh reminder of their mortality. The term "pity" mocks the shopkeepers' empty hearts. Behind the label they use for him, "the soda man" was Louis Spitzbergen, and "alive" recalls his habit of referring to the precariousness of his life without having any sense of it. "Enjoy" evokes the capacity for simple pleasure that is missing among the novel's characters. Finally, "wonderful weather" for the storekeepers is an oppressive steamy blanket; what is hell for citydwellers in their ovenlike flats is welcome in Neptune Beach. The larger circle of self-absorption dwarfs the smaller, and Lurie's epiphany is both magnified and diminished by the weight of the collective inertia.

Conclusion

One of the strengths of Fuchs's Brooklyn novels is that the social and artistic problems they address are connected by the fundamental question of whether one can know any truth with certainty. Although the three novels progressively shed their literary self-consciousness, the questions that *Summer in Williamsburg* expresses about truthful rendering persist in the other novels. Philip's scenario of a passive God—a scenario which merely extends the frontiers of his unanswered questions—becomes absorbed and obliquely rendered in the other works as an indifferent cosmos. In all three of the novels the artistic problem echoes the metaphysical one.

The first novel contains direct references to several writers and their works that give it an academic consciousness, including Eugene O'Neill (86), Dostoevsky (139), Chaucer (119), *Lady Chatterley's Lover* (157), Rabelais (157), and the novelist Joseph Hergesheimer, a contemporary of Fuchs (301). During the novel's action Philip is reading Thackeray's *Pendennis,* which is, like Philip's own story, a relatively plotless novel in which the young protagonist's ambitious uncle is a major force in his life. Philip's friend Charles borrows from a Stephen Crane poem when he replies to a woman who is trying to escape the subway crush. "This is my station. I want to get off," she cries. Charles says, "Nevertheless, the fact creates in me no sense of obligation" (325).[1] Aside from these allusions, Philip discusses philosophy and poetry with his friends, Cohen and Charles, and articulates throughout the novel his predicament as a beginning writer applying the realistic method. His quandary lies in having to select from and impose order on an infinite complexity of truths about Williamsburg and each of its people, the suicide Sussman being only one example.

Philip also ponders the more comprehensive problem of honesty in language by observing how his diction adapts to his audience (117–19). After composing a letter to Charles in such language as "characteristic," "maudlin," "rationalization," "decorously," and "notwithstanding," he is too embarrassed by its polysyllables to send it, and immediately enjoys participating in the conversation with his brother and the other thugs at their poker game, with Gilhooley speculating on shoving a pile of manure down someone's throat. At the novel's conclusion, as Philip goes about the business of waiting to observe what his fate will be, he parodies Prufrock's self-catechism with a series of paragraphs beginning with "Shall I . . ." and culminating with "And shall I, too, continue to inspect my comb in the light before my eyes for fallen hairs?" (378). As Chapter 4 of this study demonstrates, although both Philip and Fuchs have been students of life and of Professor Overstreet, Philip is not Fuchs. Philip's particular consciousness, however, gives the novel its academic tinge.

In *Homage to Blenholt,* although Max quotes extensively from Christopher Marlowe and calls his mother Mrs. MacKenzie after Thackeray's character in *The Newcomes,* he has by Ruth's account and ample other evidence never been a reader, and his bathetic use of literary heroes is part of what disqualifies him as a portrait of the artist. The dilemma that Max formulates is not Philip's, between integrity and money, but between humiliation and power, and, as solipsist, Max shares no part of his author's task of broadly comprehending and representing matters.

The character Coblentz in the second novel, like Cohen in the first, sketches out a proposed literary masterpiece—an activity which no character in *Low Company* would imagine. The only reader in that novel is Dorothy, who is engrossed in silly romances. Herbert Lurie, whose speech includes "ain't," is far removed from literary consciousness; he is informed not even by Hollywood iconography but only by common sense. Despite this gift, Lurie is not Fuchs either. The epiphany that turns him homeward does not express the entire theme of the novel, balanced as it is against an otherwise pessimistic world-picture.

Philip's craving for an ordering perspective, "something magnificent, worth enthusiasm, worth labor, to guide me for the next forty or fifty years to come," is met by Fuchs's distrust of such simplification. The reference to Ecclesiastes in the introduction to this study bears repeating; when the Preacher's inventory turns up only inequity and evanescence ("vanity"), he goes about making his account of them his life-affirming but equivocal response.

Summer in Williamsburg begins and concludes with people making assumptions about divine intentionality, but Fuchs's several glimpses of God show the Almighty's presence to be morally irrelevant. Portrayed as yet another observer-wonderer, God the Author is released by Fuchs the author from accountability. This view of matters lends even more irony to presumptions, by a pragmatic character like Papravel, of a cosmic morality. In place of the equitable governance such characters associate with "God's still being over America," Fuchs posits a multiplication of perspectives as the closest moral equivalent. Philip observes that "in Williamsburg the summer was getting over, but, on the other hand, in Tasmania it was the winter which was leaving for the soft winds of spring" (372). He has just been noticing how quickly the fire that killed Cohen and Mahler is being forgotten by their neighbors. In the reference to the South Pacific, space functions as a substitute for time in the way it calls attention to the ephemerality of all events.

Cosmos and community, Philip learns, are equally indifferent. The resumption of routine after the catastrophic fire reminds him of how life differs from fiction, which would elevate the fire to a climax with due proportion and emphasis. In ascribing significance, art is incompatible with honest telling. The ultimate irony is that the elements that define not-fiction-but-real-life for Philip, such as Sussman's inscrutable suicide, are elements in Fuchs's fiction.

Low Company has no character equipped or disposed to articulate an aesthetic dilemma, and so delusions about objectivity are obliquely dealt with. Fuchs gives full play to that craft of plotting and shaping of events which is represented in the first novel as dishonest—the control of the storyteller. On the other hand, he tries to approximate letting the story tell itself by denying saliency to any one of his characters and dispersing it among the group.

Throughout the novels, then, Fuchs permits no voice to hold authority, including the writer's. Each time a voice begins to sound salient, it is thrown into question. Shortly before Cohen's death, in one of his more discerning observations he chides Philip for ferreting at life. Philip, who has adopted Miller's general skepticism, responds credibly,

> "Oh, no, I do not ferret, I see what I see. The whole point is I don't embellish what I see with false ornamentation. Once it is false it no longer interests me. I'm willing to accept beauty and romance when I find it, but there's no necessity for kidding myself about it."

Cohen replies:

> "In that case you will never find it. This is something that does not exist by itself. The individual must have the vision. In short, Hayman, your wisdom is undergraduate and cynical." (P. 360)

If beauty does not exist by itself but rests in the observer's vision, the laboratory approach is, like Mr. Hayman's twisted apples, tasteless, dead.

The writer may be thought to have the privilege of projecting shape and value, but he also may be thought not to. Fuchs gives Mrs. Hayman the job of placing Philip's writing in its most complete perspective. In spite of himself, Philip is moved by Old Miller's Jewish funeral on a black and rainy day. The admirable rabbi is soaked, "his shoes sucking in the mud, the water penetrating until he must have felt cold and wet and miserable, but he went on stolidly uttering eeni-meenie-mini-mo to God who might have been listening but who sent down the fine rain nevertheless." Philip, feeling "oppressed, sad, and wondering," takes out a pad and begins writing. Another novelist might have allowed this act to stand as appropriate.

> "What are you doing, Philip?" [his mother] whispered reproachfully.
> "Nothing. It was an idea, it came to me when I heard the sound of the earth on the box, and I wanted to write it down so I wouldn't forget."
> Mrs. Hayman looked at him chidingly. "Do you bother with that when a man dies?" she said. (P. 194–5)

Through a tellingly placed remark by Mrs. Hayman, Fuchs goes beyond the question of which aspect to credit in an accounting of events in Williamsburg to the question of whether to substitute any account at all for the ineffable experience. The man who has just died is Philip's mentor in the scientific methodology. Not only Miller's empirical approach, however, is at doubt in this passage. Philip's eagerness to commit to record the sound of the earth on the box that contains Miller is placed in relief by his mother's more life-grounded response. This exchange is perhaps Fuchs's most compelling representation of his refusal to glorify his art.

Notes

Chapter 1. Introduction

1. Three dissertations, all in the past decade, have dealt with Fuchs's fiction. The first, by Gabriel Miller, is an introduction to Fuchs's biography and his fiction-writing career, with an emphasis on the writer's private vision. In this work, revised into a Twayne Series study now in print, Miller points out that Fuchs shares with naturalist artists the hope that their graphic portrayals will stir readers to humane responses. The second dissertation, by Mika Nye-Applebaum, attributes to Fuchs along with novelists Michael Gold and Henry Roth certain qualities of Jewish-American writers: nostalgia for the Old Country, solitariness, focus on the family, and the dreamer as schlemiel. The third dissertation, written by Paul Frederick Michelson, describes various social factors that he believes influenced Fuchs's fiction, especially Jewish history, the Depression, and the moving pictures. Michelson maintains that the background of *shtetl* culture makes Fuchs's writing "hybrid." He also looks into the development of formal techniques in the novels and short stories.

2. "Author's Preface," *The Williamsburg Trilogy* (New York: Avon, 1972), vii. An example of the laudatory yet vague reviews over the years is Hollis Alpert's piece on the three-novel edition in 1961. Alpert calls the novels "three of the best American novels of the decade, [representing] the solid achievement of an author of high stature." Calling Fuchs's gifts greater than Farrell's, Alpert raises but does not pursue the question of why Fuchs's fiction is only a minor classic. *Saturday Review,* 23 September 1961, 17–18.

3. *Summer in Williamsburg* became available in paperback in 1983. Two factors which may help to explain Fuchs's lack of renown are that in the minds of some critics his move to Hollywood in 1940 to write film scripts tainted his seriousness as a fiction writer, and that his infrequent written remarks on his work are diffident and anecdotal.

4. "Phantom Life," in *Picked-Up Pieces* (New York: Knopf, 1975), 444.

5. "In the Jungles of Brooklyn," *Standards: A Chronicle of Books for Our Time* (New York: Horizon Press, 1966), 46.

6. "The End of a Literary Decade," *American Mercury* 48 (December 1939): 408.

7. "Edmund Wilson's Political Decade," in *Literature at the Barricades: The American Writer in the 1930s,* ed. Ralph Bogardus and Fred Hobson, Fifth Alabama Symposium of English and American Literature (University: Alabama University Press), 177.

8. "American Fiction: The Major Trend," in *Proletarian Literature in the U.S.: An Anthology,* ed. Hicks et al. (New York: International Publishers, 1935), 360.

9. *The American Jitters: A Year of the Slump* (1932; reprint, Freeport, N.Y.: Books for Libraries Press, 1968).

10. Daniel Aaron, *The Triple Thinkers: Ten Essays on Literature* (New York: Harcourt, Brace, 1938), 241.

11. "The Thirties in Retrospect," in *Literature at the Barricades: The American Writer in the 1930s,* ed. Bogardus and Hobson, 27.

12. In his recent "Intellectual Autobiography," *A Margin of Hope,* Howe ascribes his harsh remarks on Fuchs in *Commentary* of July 1948 to his own unresolved conflicts about writing for a bourgeois journal (San Diego: Harcourt Brace Jovanovich, 1982), 114.

13. *Proletarian Writers of the Thirties* (Carbondale: Southern Illinois University Press, 1968), 5.

14. "James T. Farrell and the Thirties," in *Literature at the Barricades: The American Writer in the 1930s,* ed. Bogardus and Hobson, 73.

15. "The End of a Literary Decade," 413–15.

16. *Classics and Commercials: A Literary Chronicle of the Forties* (New York: Farrar, Straus, 1950), 168–70.

17. "Child of Sorrow," *The New Republic,* 24 February 1937, 89–90.

18. *Nathanael West,* University of Minnesota Pamphlets of American Writers, no. 21 (Minneapolis: University of Minnesota Press, 1962), 27–28.

19. A reference to a 1940 article in *The New Republic,* "The Boys in the Back Room: James M. Cain and John O'Hara," which gave the first serious attention to the genre (11 November 1940): 665–66. Commentary on other writers was added for the 1950 reprint in *Classics and Commercials.*

20. *James M. Cain* (New York: Twayne, 1970), throughout.

21. *On Native Ground* (New York: Reynal and Hitchcock, 1942), 301–3.

22. Madden, *James M. Cain,* 164–65.

23. *World of Our Fathers* (New York: Harcourt Brace Jovanovich, 1976), 591.

24. *Rediscoveries* (New York: Crown, 1971), 68; "Homage to Blenholt," *Rediscoveries,* 67.

25. A valuable discussion is Bonny Lyons's chapter, "*Call It Sleep* As A Jewish Novel," in *Henry Roth: The Man And His Work* (New York: Cooper Square, 1976), 125–34.

26. In Howe's words, for example, the history of *Winesburg* studies "is a curious instance of the way criticism, with its passion for 'placing,' can reduce a writer to harmless irrelevance," *Sherwood Anderson* (New York: William Sloan, 1951), 98. Jeanne Braham maintains in a recent study that Saul Bellow's American intellectual heritage has been overshadowed by critical emphasis on his Jewish tradition (*A Sort of Columbus: The American Voyages of Saul Bellow's Fiction* (Athens: University of Georgia, 1984). Daniel Fuchs (b. 1934, not related to the novelist) makes a similar case for placing Bellow in a broader context, in *Saul Bellow: Vision and Revision* (Durham: Duke University Press, 1984).

27. "Cold War Blues: Notes on the Culture of the Fifties," *Partisan Review* 41, no. 1 (1974): 42.

28. For example, Bernard Sherman's *The Invention of the Jew: Jewish-American Education Novels (1916–1964)* (New York: A. S. Barnes, 1969), and Leon Israel Yudkin's *Jewish Writing and Identity in the Twentieth Century* (New York: St. Martin's, 1982), 40–41. Sherman calls Fuchs a one-book novelist, 72.

29. Letter to M. Krafchick, 30 May 1984.

30. Leslie Fiedler writes that "the '30's, not only in America (where Daniel Fuchs and Henry Roth . . . are outstanding figures) but everywhere, is a period

especially favorable for the Jewish writer bent on universalizing his own experience into a symbol of life in the Western world. More and more it has seemed to such writers that what they in their exile and urbanization have long been, Western man in general is becoming," in *Love and Death in the American Novel* (New York: Stein and Day, 1966), 487. For the controversy about what Fiedler calls Arthur Miller's "crypto-Jewish characters," see Fiedler, *Waiting for the End* (New York: Stein and Day, 1964), 91; Mary McCarthy, *Sights and Spectacles* (London: William Heinemann, 1959), xxv; and Robert A. Martin, "The Creative Experience of Arthur Miller: An Interview," *Educational Theatre Journal* (October 1969): 315.

31. Fuchs objected to the decision to publish the novels as a trilogy, according to his son, Jacob Fuchs, in an interview on 31 January 1985.

32. "Last Exit to L. A.," *New York Review of Books,* 6 December 1979, 10.

33. *The American Writer and the Great Depression* (Indianapolis, Ind.: Bobbs-Merrill, 1966), xxxiv.

34. Daniel Fuchs, *Summer in Williamsburg,* in *3 Novels by Daniel Fuchs* (New York: Basic Books, 1961), 242–43. All subsequent references are cited in the text and refer to this edition. The paperback edition, entitled *The Williamsburg Trilogy* (New York: Basic Books, 1972), uses the same pagination.

35. "Proletarian Literature: A Political Autopsy," in *Literature and the Sixth Sense* (Boston: Houghton Mifflin, 1969), 8.

36. Howe wrote in *Commentary* in 1948 that "Fuchs, having decided not to become a literary Max Balkan, has largely withdrawn his sympathy from his characters." Fuchs's one surpassing truth, according to that article, is that "all human beings are *dreck,*" in "Daniel Fuchs: Escape From Williamsburg—The Fate of Talent in America," *Commentary,* July 1948, 32–33. In *Harpers* in 1971, Howe observes that compassion does enter Fuchs's writing ("Books: *West of the Rockies,*" *Harpers,* June 1971, 89). And in *World of Our Fathers* (1976) Howe refers to the "wry and disenchanted tenderness" that Fuchs brings to the Jewish experience (591).

37. *Rediscoveries,* 69.

38. "Child of Sorrow," 90.

39. "The Down Syndrome," *Times Literary Supplement,* 18 April 1980, 431. This review of Fuchs's collection of short stories, *The Apathetic Bookie Joint,* is discerning about Fuchs's fiction in general.

40. "The Rat Race on the Brooklyn Track," *New York Times Book Review,* 10 September 1961, 22.

41. "Soda Parlor in Brooklyn," *The Nation,* 27 February 1937, 244. Farrell commends Fuchs's "genuine respect for his characters."

42. Richard Elman, "Dr. Fuchs' Hollywood Brother," *The Nation,* 26 January 1980, 88.

43. "Mr. Eliot, Mr. Wyndham Lewis and Lawrence," in *The Common Pursuit* (London: Chatto and Windus, 1952), 241.

Chapter 2. The Gangster as Theme

1. From about 1896 to 1925 the term "gangster" referred to a political reprobate. After 1925 it came to designate a professional criminal who works with associates in a structured organization. The term gained currency only in the thirties. Cf. H. L. Mencken, *The American Language: An Inquiry Into the Development of English in the United States,* supplement 1 (New York: Alfred A. Knopf, 1956), 359, and Harold Wentworth and Stuart Berg Flexner, *Dictionary of American Slang* (New York: Thomas Y. Crowell, 1967), 208.

2. Daniel Fuchs, *Homage to Blenholt,* in *3 Novels by Daniel Fuchs* (New York: Basic Books, 1961), 215. All further references to the novel are cited in the text and refer to this edition.

3. Daniel Fuchs, *Low Company,* in *3 Novels by Daniel Fuchs* (New York: Basic Books, 1961). All further references to the novel are cited in the text and refer to this edition.

4. Interview with Jacob Fuchs, January 30, 1985.

5. Leo Katchen, *The Big Bankroll* (New York: 1958), 231.

6. Jenna Weissman Joselit, *Our Gang: Jewish Crime and the New York Jewish Community, 1900–1940* (Bloomington: Indiana University Press, 1983), 154–55.

7. Letter to M. Krafchick, 12 August 1985.

8. Arthur Knight, *The Liveliest Art: A Panoramic History of the Movies* (New York: Mentor, 1979), 261.

9. Stuart M. Kaminsky, *American Film Genres: Approaches to a Critical Theory of Popular Film* (New York: Dell, 1974), 33.

10. Robert Warshow, "The Gangster As Tragic Hero," in *The Immediate Experience* (New York: Atheneum Press, 1970), 132–33.

11. Kaminsky, *American Film Genres,* 24.

12. Knight, *The Liveliest Art,* 261.

13. Kaminsky, *American Film Genres,* 41.

Chapter 3. Style and Technique: Doubting Perspectives

1. Yudkin writes, for example, about *Summer in Williamsburg,* "There is just observation," in *Jewish Writing and Identity in the Twentieth Century,* 41.

2. George J. Becker, *Master European Realists of the Nineteenth Century* (New York: Frederick Ungar, 1982), 7.

3. Bernard Sherman, for example, calls Philip the narrator-protagonist in *The Invention of the Jew: Jewish-American Education Novels (1916–1964),* 104.

4. Fuchs says that he had read the entire Romains series and was more interested in their form than their theory. He compares Romains's form to that of Dickens and Thackeray. (Letter to M. Krafchick, 9 February 1985.)

5. In this respect it is related as well to continental experiments in expressionism, such as the plays of Ernst Toller and Karel Capek, which used types for characters, and the epic drama of Bertold Brecht.

6. P. J. Norrish, *Drama of the Group: A Study of Unanism in the Plays of Jules Romains* (Cambridge: Cambridge University Press, 1958), 8.

7. *Miss Lonelyhearts,* in *The Complete Works of Nathanael West,* with an Introduction by Alan Ross (New York: Farrar, Straus and Giroux, 1957), 114.

8. *E. W. Howe* (New York: Twayne, 1972), 76–78.

9. Introduction, *Windy McPherson's Son* (Chicago: University of Chicago Press, 1965), xvi.

10. *Comedy High and Low: An Introduction to the Experience of Comedy* (New York: Oxford University Press, 1978), 12. Ruth Gay writes: "In America there was hope, opportunity, even prosperity. Soft beds, enough food, safety. This was not *golus* [exile] in its heartrending, ultimate blackness. If the truth be told, this was Paradise, and the only way to resolve this contradiction was humor," in "Inventing the Shtetl," *American Scholar* (Summer 1984): 348.

11. Allen Guttman, *The Jewish Writer in America: Assimilation and the Crisis of Identity* (New York: Oxford University Press, 1971), 47.

12. *Symbolisme et interpretation* (Paris: Editions du Seuil, 1978), 82.

13. The butterfly, like Steinbeck's turtle crossing the road, is a persistent force for survival, but more fragile, ephemeral, and dislocated. The image occurs also in one of Fuchs's stories, "A Clean Quiet House" (*The New Yorker,* 30 May 1942).

14. As one is reminded in *Summer in Williamsburg,* moviegoers used to shout at those obstructing their view, "Sit down! Your father wasn't a glazier!" Further play on Shubunka's paternity is in the fact that adding silver (money) to glass produces mirror.

15. (New York: Avon, 1972), 222.

Chapter 4. *Summer in Williamsburg*

1. When Fuchs, at only twenty-two, submitted a piece to the *New Republic,* its editor, Malcolm Cowley, encouraged him to expand it into a novel. For publication Fuchs shortened the piece, which he had originally called "A Brooklyn Boyhood," and retitled it "Where Al Capone Grew Up" (9 September 1931, 95–97). The article is the early version of what would become *Summer in Williamsburg.* In confining the novel's time to the summer months he omitted the story's descriptions of pogromlike attacks on Jews at Halloween, and he never again made anti-Semitism an important element in his work.

2. Brom Weber, *Sherwood Anderson* (Minneapolis: University of Minnesota Press, 1964), 35.

3. *Winesburg, Ohio* (New York: Penguin, 1984), 36.

4. By montage I mean the arrangement of images not in order to advance the story's linear sequence but to evoke some emotional or intellectual connection in the spectator. Montage is a means of arresting an incongruity, striking it home through movement rather than through discourse. As Sergei Eisenstein demonstrates in his study of Dickens, fiction writers anticipated the cinema in using scenic juxtaposition to convey meaning ("Dickens, Griffith, and the Film Today," in *Film Form: Essays in Film Theory* and *The Film Sense,* ed. and trans. Jay Leyda [New York: Meridian Press, 1960], 195–255). It is likely, nonetheless, that Fuchs's frequent attendance at movies helped him develop the skill of fictive montage.

5. Michelson, the only commentator who refers to this scene, regards it as gratuitous, 210.

6. Lida Newberry, ed., *New Jersey: A Guide to Its Present and Past* (New York: Hastings House, 1977), 584–85.

Chapter 5. *Homage to Blenholt*

1. Exceptions are Chapter 7, at Blenholt's funeral, Chapter 10, at the cigar store where Coblenz bets on horses, and some few passages such as Ruth's experience at the hairdresser's and Max's recalled visit to the Onagonda Onion Corporation office.

2. Gabriel Miller compares Fuchs's comedy in *Homage to Blenholt* with conventions of eighteenth- and nineteenth-century social comedies, in *Daniel Fuchs* (Boston: Twayne, 1979), 65–66. For useful reviews of theories and conventions of comedy see R. J. Dorius, "Comedy," in *Princeton Encyclopedia of Poetry and Poetics,* ed. Alex Preminger (Princeton: Princeton University Press, 1974), 143–47, and Wylie Sypher, "The Meanings of Comedy," in *Comedy* (Garden City, N. Y.: Doubleday, 1956), 193–255.

3. "Daniel Fuchs: Chronicler of Williamsburg," 165.

4. Aside from hesitating, Max also balks in the sense of blundering, and is balked, or frustrated.

5. Interview with Jacob Fuchs, 30 January 1985.

Chapter 6. *Low Company*

1. "Sonny's Blues," in *Going to Meet the Man* (*Partisan Review,* Summer 1957; reprint, New York: Dial Press, 1965), 127.

2. *The Monster and Other Stories* (*Collier's Weekly,* 26 November, 3 December 1898; reprint, New York: Harper & Brothers, 1899).

3. *High Holiday Prayer Book* (Hartford, Conn.: Prayer Book Press, 1939), 433.

4. A third significance may be found in the Mishna Yoma, Chapter 8: "For transgressions between man and God, repentance on Yom Kippur brings atonement, but for transgressions between man and man, Yom Kippur brings no atonement until the injured party is appeased." This passage is consistent with Fuchs's humanistic treatment of the theme of transgression.

5. John F. Kasson, *Amusing the Million: Coney Island at the Turn of the Century* (New York: Hill and Wang, 1978), 88.

6. Richard Cox, "Coney Island: Urban Symbol in American Art," in *Brooklyn, USA: The Fourth Largest City in America,* ed. Rita Seiden Miller (New York: Brooklyn College Press, 1979), 137–38.

7. Cox, "Coney Island," 143.

8. Kasson, *Amusing the Million,* 98.

9. Ronald Sanders, *Reflections on a Teapot* (New York: Harper and Row, 1972), 379.

10. Oliver Pilat and Jo Ranson (New York: Doubleday, Doran, 1941), 316.

11. *Daniel Fuchs* (Boston: Twayne, 1979), 97.

12. *Renascence,* 13 (1961), 70.

13. Fuchs writes that he thinks he saw the name in a taxi once. Letter to M. Krafchick, 9 February 1985.

14. *The American Novel and its Tradition* (New York: Doubleday, 1957), 191.

15. Michelson, in his dissertation, comments that Herbert Lurie's change from callousness to compassion is too sudden and abstract to be convincing. He sees Lurie's moral lesson as futile in the context of Neptune's deep-seated venality. "Either Fuchs believed in that venality more deeply than he did in the values he recommends to combat it, or he simply insisted on the malaise to the point that it makes virtue seem ineffective" (224). The limited magnitude of Lurie's conversion, however, may convey instead the idea that an awakening to compassion of only one person can be a basis for hope.

Chapter 7. Conclusion

1. "A Man Said to the Universe," in *The Complete Poems of Stephen Crane,* ed. Joseph Katz (Ithaca: Cornell University Press, 1972), 102:

> A man said to the universe:
> "Sir, I exist!"
> "However," replied the universe,
> "The fact has not created in me
> A sense of obligation."

Select Bibliography

Aaron, Daniel. "Edmund Wilson's Political Decade." In *Literature at the Barricades: The American Writer in the 1930s,* edited by Ralph Bogardus and Fred Hobson. Fifth Alabama Symposium of English and American Literature. University: Alabama University Press, 1982.

Alpert, Hollis. "The Southside Story." Review of *3 Novels by Daniel Fuchs. The Saturday Review of Literature,* 23 September 1961, 17–18.

Anderson, Sherwood. *Winesburg, Ohio.* New York: Penguin, 1984.

Baldwin, James. "Sonny's Blues." In *Going to Meet the Man.* New York: Dial Press, 1965. Reprinted from *Partisan Review* (Summer 1957).

Beaver, Harold. "The Down Syndrome." *Times Literary Supplement,* 18 April 1980, 431.

Becker, George J. *Master European Realists of the Nineteenth Century.* New York: Frederick Ungar, 1982.

Bergman, Andrew. "The Gangsters." In *We're In the Money.* New York: New York University Press, 1971.

Boak, Denis. *Jules Romains.* New York: Twayne, 1974.

Braham, Jeanne. *A Sort of Columbus: The American Voyage of Saul Bellow's Fiction.* Athens: University of Georgia Press, 1984.

Burnett, William Riley. *Little Caesar.* New York: The Dial Press, 1929.

Cahan, Abraham. *The Rise of David Levinsky.* New York: Harper and Brothers, 1917.

Cain, James N. *The Butterfly.* New York: Alfred A. Knopf, 1947.

Chametzky, Jules. *From the Ghetto: The Fiction of Abraham Cahan.* Amherst: The University of Masssachusetts Press, 1977.

―――. "Main Currents in American Jewish Literature from the 1880's to the 1950's (and Beyond)." *Ethnic Groups* 4, nos. 1–2 (1982): 85–101.

Charney, Maurice. *Comedy High and Low: An Introduction to the Experience of Comedy.* New York: Oxford University Press, 1978.

Chase, Richard. *The American Novel and Its Tradition.* New York: Doubleday, 1957.

Cox, Richard. "Coney Island: Urban Symbol in American Art." In *Brooklyn, USA: The Fourth Largest City in America,* edited by Rita Seiden Miller. New York: Brooklyn College Press, 1979.

Crane, Stephen. "The Blue Hotel." In *The Monster and Other Stories.* New York and London: Harper & Brothers, 1899. Reprinted from *Collier's Weekly,* 26 November, 3 December 1898.

————. "A Man Said to the Universe." *The Complete Poems of Stephen Crane.* Edited by Joseph Katz. Ithaca: Cornell University Press, 1972, 102.

Dardis, Tom. *Some Time in the Sun.* New York: Charles Scribner's Sons, 1976.

Davis, Robert Gorham. "The Rat Race on the Brooklyn Track." *New York Times Book Review,* 10 September 1961, 22.

Dickstein, Morris. "Cold War Blues: Notes on the Culture of the Fifties." *Partisan Review,* 41, no. 1 (1974): 30–53.

Dorius, R. J. "Comedy." In *Princeton Encyclopedia of Poetry and Poetics,* edited by Alex Preminger. Princeton: Princeton University Press, 1974.

Eisenstein, Sergei. "Dickens, Griffith, and the Film Today." In *Film Form: Essays in Film Theory* and *The Film Sense,* edited and translated by Jay Leyda, 195–255. New York: Meridian, 1960.

Eliot, T. S. *The Waste Land.* In *The Complete Poems and Plays.* New York: Harcourt, Brace, 1952.

Elman, Richard. "Dr. Fuchs' Hollywood Brother." *The Nation,* 26 January 1980, 88.

Farrell, James T. "The End of a Literary Decade." *American Mercury* 48 (December 1939): 408–15. Reprinted in *Literature at the Barricades: The American Writer in the 1930s,* edited by Ralph Bogardus and Fred Hobson. Fifth Alabama Symposium of English and American Literature. University: Alabama University Press, 1982.

————. *James T. Farrell: Literary Essays 1954–74.* Edited by Jack Alan Robbins. Port Washington, N.Y.: Kennekat, 1976.

————. "Soda Parlor in Brooklyn." Review of *Low Company,* by Daniel Fuchs. *The Nation,* 27 February 1937, 244.

Fiedler, Leslie. *Love and Death in the American Novel.* New York: Stein and Day, 1966.

————. *Waiting for the End.* New York: Stein and Day, 1964.

Fuchs, Daniel. *The Apathetic Bookie Joint.* New York: Methuen, 1979.

————. "A Clean Quiet House." *New Yorker,* 30 May 1942. Reprinted in *The Apathetic Bookie Joint,* 31–38. New York: Methuen, 1979.

————. Letter to M. Krafchick, 30 May 1984.

————. Letter to M. Krafchick, 9 February 1985.

————. Letter to M. Krafchick, 12 August 1985.

————. *3 Novels by Daniel Fuchs: Summer in Williamsburg; Homage to Blenholt; Low Company.* New York: Basic Books, 1961.

————. *West of the Rockies.* New York: Alfred A. Knopf, 1971.

————. "Where Al Capone Grew Up." *The New Republic,* 9 September 1931, 95–97.

Fuchs, Daniel (1934–). *Saul Bellow: Vision and Revision.* Durham: Duke University Press, 1984.

Fuchs, Jacob. Interview with M. Krafchick, 31 January 1985.

Gabree, John. *Gangsters from Little Caesar to The Godfather.* New York: Pyramid, 1973.

Gay, Ruth. "Inventing the Shtetl." *American Scholar* (Summer 1984): 329–49.

Glazer, Nathan, and Daniel Patrick Moynihan. *Beyond the Melting Pot.* Cambridge: The M. I. T. Press, 1967.

Gold, Michael. *Jews without Money.* New York: Avon, 1972.

Guttman, Allen. *The Jewish Writer in America: Assimilation and the Crisis of Identity.* New York: Oxford University Press, 1971.

Halper, Albert. "Child of Sorrow." Review of *Low Company,* by Daniel Fuchs. *The New Republic,* 24 February 1937, 89–90.

Harrington, Michael. Afterword to *Jews without Money,* by Michael Gold. New York: Avon, 1972.

Hicks, Granville. "American Fiction: The Major Trend." In *Proletarian Literature in the U.S.: An Anthology,* edited by Granville Hicks et al. New York: International Publishers, 1935.

Howe, E. W. *The Story of a Country Town.* Boston and New York: Houghton, Mifflin and Company, 1884.

Howe, Irving. "Books: *West of the Rockies.*" *Harpers,* June 1971, 89.

———. "Daniel Fuchs: Escape from Williamsburg—The Fate of Talent in America." *Commentary,* July 1948, 29–34.

———. "Last Exit to L.A." *New York Review of Books,* 6 December 1979, 10.

———. *A Margin of Hope.* San Diego: Harcourt Brace Jovanovich, 1982.

———. *Sherwood Anderson.* New York: William Sloane, 1951.

———. "The Thirties in Retrospect." In *Literature at the Barricades: The American Writer in the 1930s,* edited by Ralph Bogardus and Fred Hobson. Fifth Alabama Symposium of English and American Literature. University: Alabama University Press, 1982.

———. *World of Our Fathers.* New York: Harcourt Brace Jovanovich, 1976.

Hyman, Stanley Edgar. "In the Jungles of Brooklyn." In *Standards: A Chronicle of Books for Our Time.* New York: Horizon Press, 1966.

———. *Nathanael West.* University of Minnesota Pamphlet of American Writers, no. 21. Minneapolis: University of Minnesota Press, 1962.

Joselit, Jenna Weissman. *Our Gang: Jewish Crime and the New York Jewish Community, 1900–1940.* Bloomington: Indiana University Press, 1983.

Kaminsky, Stuart M. *American Film Genres: Approaches to a Critical Theory of Popular Film.* New York: Dell, 1974.

Kasson, John F. *Amusing the Million: Coney Island at the Turn of the Century.* American Century Series. New York: Hill and Wang, 1978.

Katcher, Leo. *The Big Bankroll: The Life and Times of Arnold Rothstein.* New York: Harper, 1959.

Kazin, Alfred. *Bright Book of Life: American Novelists and Storytellers from Hemingway to Mailer.* Boston: Little, Brown, 1971.

———. *Contemporaries, from the 19th Century to the Present.* New York: Horizon Press, 1982.

———. *On Native Grounds: An Interpretation of Modern American Prose Literature.* New York: Reynal and Hitchcock, 1942.

———. *Proletarian Writers of the Thirties.* Carbondale and Edwardsville: Southern Illinois University Press, 1968.

———, ed. *Nathanael West: The Cheaters and the Cheated: A Collection of Critical Essays.* Deland, Fla.: Everett/Edwards, Inc., 1973.

Knight, Arthur. *The Liveliest Art: A Panoramic History of the Movies.* New York: MacMillan, 1957.

Leavis, F. R. "Mr. Eliot, Mr. Wyndham Lewis and Lawrence." In *The Common Pursuit*. London: Chatto & Windus, 1952.

Lyons, Bonny. "*Call It Sleep* as a Jewish Novel." In *Henry Roth: The Man and His Work*. New York: Cooper Square, 1976.

McCarthy, Mary. *Sights and Spectacles*. London: William Heinemann, 1959.

Madden, David. *James M. Cain*. New York: Twayne, 1970.

————, ed. *Rediscoveries: Informal Essays in Which Well-Known Novelists Rediscover Neglected Works of Fiction by One of Their Favorite Authors*. New York: Crown, 1971.

Martin, Robert A. "The Creative Experience of Arthur Miller: An Interview." *Educational Theatre Journal* (October 1969): 310–17.

Mencken, H. L. *The American Language: An Inquiry into the Development of English in the United States,* supplement 1. New York: Alfred A. Knopf, 1956.

Michelson, Paul Frederick. "Daniel Fuchs: Chronicler of Williamsburg." Ph.D. diss., Washington State University, 1981.

Miller, Gabriel. "The Butterfly in the Subway: The Fiction of Daniel Fuchs." Ph.D. diss., Brown University, 1975.

————. *Daniel Fuchs*. Boston: Twayne, 1979.

————. *Screening the Novel: Rediscovered American Fiction in Film*. New York: Frederick Ungar, 1980.

————. "Screenwriter Daniel Fuchs: A Creed Grows in Brooklyn." *Los Angeles Times Book Review,* 17 April 1977, 3.

Miller, Rita Seiden, ed. *Brooklyn, USA: The Fourth Largest City in America*. New York: Brooklyn College Press, 1979.

Moore, Deborah Dash. *At Home in America: Second Generation New York Jews*. New York: Columbia University Press, 1981.

Morris, Wright. Introduction to *Windy McPherson's Son,* by Sherwood Anderson. Chicago: University of Chicago Press, 1965.

Murphy, Mary Ellen, Mark Murphy, and Ralph Foster Weld. *A Treasury of Brooklyn*. New York: William Sloane Associates, 1949.

Newberry, Lida, ed. *New Jersey: A Guide to Its Present and Past*. New York: Hastings House, 1977.

Norrish, P. J. *Drama of the Group: A Study of Unanism in the Plays of Jules Romains*. Cambridge: Cambridge University Press, 1958.

Nye-Applebaum, Mika. "Restructuring the Beginning. Three Writers in the 30's: The Novels of Michael Gold, Henry Roth and Daniel Fuchs." Ph.D. diss., State University of New York at Buffalo, 1980.

Ornitz, Samuel B. *Haunch, Paunch and Jowl: An Anonymous Autobiography*. New York: Boni and Liveright, 1923.

Peary, Gerald. "Rico Rising: Little Caesar Takes Over the Screen." In *The Classic American Novel and the Movies*. New York: Frederick Ungar, 1977.

Pells, Richard H. *Radical Visions and American Dreams*. New York: Harper & Row, 1973.

Phillips, William, and Philip Rahv. "In Retrospect: Ten Years of *Partisan Review*." In *The Partisan Reader*. New York: The Dial Press, 1946.

Pilat, Oliver, and Jo Ranson. *Sodom by the Sea: An Affectionate History of Coney Island*. New York: Doubleday, Doran, 1941.

Pinsker, Sanford. *The Schlemiel as Metaphor: Studies in the Yiddish and American Jewish Novel.* Crosscurrents/Modern Critiques. Carbondale: Southern Illinois University Press, 1971.

Pizer, Donald. "James T. Farrell and the Thirties." In *Literature at the Barricades: The American Writer in the 1930s,* edited by Ralph Bogardus and Fred Hobson. Fifth Alabama Symposium of English and American Literature. University: Alabama University Press, 1982.

Rahv, Philip. *Literature and the Sixth Sense.* Boston: Houghton Mifflin, 1969.

———. "Notes on the Decline of Naturalism." In *Documents of Modern Literary Naturalism,* edited by George J. Becker. Princeton: Princeton University Press, 1963.

———. "Proletarian Literature: A Political Autopsy." *Southern Review* 4 (1940): 617.

Rosenberg, Bernard, and Ernest Goldstein. *Creators and Disturbers: Reminiscences by Jewish Intellectuals of New York.* New York: Columbia University Press, 1982.

Roth, Henry. *Call It Sleep.* New York: Robert O. Ballou, 1934.

Sackett, S. J. *E. W. Howe.* New York: Twayne, 1972.

Salzman, Jack. *Years of Protest: A Collection of American Writings of the 1930s.* New York: Western Publishing Company (Pegasus), 1967.

Sanders, Ronald. *Reflections on a Teapot.* New York: Harper and Row, 1972.

Shaw, Irwin. "Homage to Blenholt." In *Rediscoveries,* edited by David Madden. New York: Crown, 1971.

Sherman, Bernard. *The Invention of the Jew: Jewish-American Education Novels (1916–1964)* New York: Barnes, 1969.

Siegel, Ben. "Fuchs, Daniel." In *Contemporary Novelists,* edited by James Vinson. New York: St. Martin's Press, 1972.

Silverman, Rabbi Morris. *High Holiday Prayer Book.* Hartford, Conn.: Prayer Book Press, 1939.

Solomon, Stanley J. *The Film Idea.* New York: Harcourt Brace Jovanovich, 1972.

Steinbeck, John. *The Grapes of Wrath.* New York: Viking Press, 1939.

Strauss, Harold. "*Low Company* and Other Recent Works of Fiction." *New York Times Book Review,* 28 February 1937, 6.

Swados, Harvey. *The American Writer and the Great Depression.* Indianapolis, Ind.: Bobbs-Merrill, 1966.

Sypher, Wylie. "The Meanings of Comedy." In *Comedy,* edited by Wylie Sypher. Garden City, N.Y.: Doubleday, 1956.

Todorov, Tzvetan. *Symbolisme et interpretation.* Paris: Editions du Seuil, 1978.

Updike, John. Afterword to *West of the Rockies.* New York: Popular Library, 1971.

———. "Phantom Life." In *Picked-Up Pieces.* New York: Knopf, 1975.

Volpe, Edmond L. "The Waste Land of Nathanael West." *Renascence* 13 (1961): 69.

Wagenknecht, Edward. *Cavalcade of the American Novel.* New York: Henry Holt, 1952.

Warshow, Robert. "The Gangster as Tragic Hero." In *The Immediate Experience.* Garden City, N.Y.: Doubleday, 1962.

Weber, Brom. *Sherwood Anderson*. Minneapolis: University of Minnesota Press, 1964.

Wentworth, Harold and Stuart Berg Flexner. *Dictionary of American Slang*. New York: Thomas Y. Crowell, 1967.

West, Nathanael. *The Complete Works*. New York: Farrar, Straus and Giroux, 1957.

Wilson, Edmund. *The American Jitters: A Year of the Slump*. 1932. Reprint. Freeport, N. Y.: Books for Libraries Press, 1968.

―――. *Classics and Commercials: A Literary Chronicle of the Forties*. New York: Farrar, Straus, 1950.

―――. *The Triple Thinkers: Ten Essays on Literature*. New York: Harcourt, Brace, 1938.

Winchell, Mark Royden. *Horace McCoy*. Boise, Idaho: Boise State University Press, 1982.

Yudkin, Leon Israel. *Jewish Writing and Identity in the Twentieth Century*. New York: St. Martin's Press, 1982.

Index

Aaron, Daniel, 12
Absurdist vision, 65
Algren, Nelson, 19
Ambiguity: as device and metaphysic, 19, 20, 21, 32, 34, 41, 44, 49, 95
Ambivalence, 19, 21, 28, 29, 74, 79, 88
American culture, 69–71, 79
American dream (promise), 15, 18–19, 22, 24, 28, 29, 40, 66, 69, 70, 71, 77. *See also* Horatio Alger myth
American Tragedy, An (Dreiser), 91
Anastasia, Albert, 26
Anderson, Sherwood, 16, 17, 21, 36, 40, 41, 51, 59. See also *Winesburg, Ohio*
Anticapitalism: failing of, 20
Art as "concocted ordering," 34, 63, 102
Arthur (character), 90–92
Artist: as liar, 53, 71, 102; and problems of form, 41, 54, 55, 62, 63, 100, 102
Authorial distance, 72
Awake and Sing (Odets), 41, 76

Balance of competing sympathies, 34, 41, 49, 50, 79, 88, 94, 97. *See also* Ambivalence
Balkan, Crenya (character), 75–76
Balkan, Label (character), 69, 71
Balkan, Max (character), 31–32, 40, 64–67, 70–74, 78; bizarre gait of, 64, 72
Balzac, Honoré de, 39
Beaver, Harold, 20
Becker, George: on European realism, 35
Bellow, Saul, 12, 16, 21
Betrayals, 22, 59, 63, 87–88
Bildungsroman hero, 37, 64
Black Mask, 14
Blenholt (character), 31, 66
Bostonians, The (James), 41

"Boys in the Back Room" (Wilson), 14
Broken legs: as symbol, 48
Brooklyn environment, 25, 51, 61, 84
Buchalter, Louis "Lepke," 26
Business as crime, 20, 22, 24, 25, 30–31, 33. *See also* Crime as business
Butterfly: as symbol, 44, 78
Butterfly, The (Cain), 15

Cain, James M., 13, 14, 15
Capitalism, 22, 71; artist and, 12, 13; failings of, 20
Capra, Frank, 27
Certainties: questioning of, 11, 46, 49, 100. *See also* Skepticism
Chandler, Raymond, 14
Chase, Richard, 94
Chaucer, Geoffrey, 30, 38, 100
Chekhov, Anton, 12
Children: role of, 83
Circle as structure: *Low Company,* 32, 39, 49, 62, 63, 95; *Summer in Williamsburg,* 62–63
Circle of characters, 82, 92–93, 96, 98, 99
Classifications, period and genre, 13–14, 16
Coblenz (character), 68, 74–75, 78–79
Cohen (character), 37
"Collecting" (empirical observation), 36, 37, 38, 43, 51, 52, 54, 56, 60
Collective protagonist, 35, 39, 55, 81; distinguished from multiple, 39. *See also* Protagonists
Combination, the, 24, 25, 26, 35. *See also* Syndicate, the
Comedy, 57, 64, 67, 74, 78, 79, 92; Jewish, 42
Comic conventions, 64
Comic treatment, 33, 38, 73, 76
Communal responsibility, 80–81

Communism, 37, 48, 71; and art, 12, 13
Community: claims of, 39, 40, 67; as microcosm, 41; spirit of, 35; as protagonist, 55, 81. *See also* Collective protagonist
Comprehensiveness, 34, 39, 49, 52, 56, 101–2
Coney Island, 26; as apocalyptic microcosm, 84–85
Crane, Stephen, 21, 80, 100
Credibility: distribution of, 20, 34, 35, 46, 102–3
Crime as business, 22, 24, 25, 26, 30, 33. *See also* Business as crime; Syndicate, the
Criticism, radical, 13; political preoccupation of, 12–14

Dahlberg, Edward, 19
Davis, Robert Gorham, 20
Day of the Locust (West), 39, 97
Dead End (Kingsley), 41
Death, 54, 59
Death of a Salesman (Miller), 16
Depression era, 12, 13, 14, 17–18, 29
Determinism, 32, 34, 60, 80, 97
Deus ex machina, 68
Dickstein, Morris, 16
Diction, 30, 100
Disagreeable characters, 48–49, 56, 57–58
Documentary technique, 40. *See also* Realism: American
Doors: as symbol, 44, 45, 46
Dos Passos, John, 41
Dostoevsky, Fyodor, 12, 100
Drama: Elizabethan, 30, 38; multiple protagonist in, 41
Dreiser, Theodore, 41, 91
Durrenmatt, Friedrich, 39

Ecclesiastes, 21, 101
Education novel, 20, 36, 38
Eliot, T. S., 21, 43, 86
Empiricism, 51, 52, 63, 103. *See also* "Collecting"
Employment, 18, 30, 70
Epigraph, in *Low Company*, 49, 81, 83, 86, 89, 93
Ethnic identity: absence of, in *Low Company*, 81–82

Fable: *Low Company* as, 17
Falling: as motif, 44, 48, 78
Farce, 64, 78
Farrell, James T., 12, 13, 20, 86, 97
Faulkner, William, 12, 14, 15, 16, 21
Fitzgerald, F. Scott, 14, 25
Focus: distribution of, 35, 36–37, 39, 41, 46, 65
Foils, 37
Frame, 47, 55
Fuchs, Daniel: boyhood of, 51; brothers of, 25, 48, 74; and critics, 11, 12, 16, 20, 42, 44, 51; and emphasis on character, 16; first published article of, 25; as individualistic writer, 13; influences on, 25, 27, 39; his interest in gangster, 25; on Jewishness, 16; as Jewish novelist, 11, 83; his move to Hollywood, 13, 27; *The New Yorker*, his stories in, 11; and politics, absence of, 12; as progenitor of modern Jewish-American writers, 16; as social novelist, 11, 17, 19, 20, 21; as teacher in Coney Island, 82

"Ganev" (thief), 18, 71
Gangster, 20; in American mythology, 22; emblem for Depression, 29; Fuchs's acquaintance with, 25, 26–27; Fuchs's various uses of, 12, 29–32; Hollywood's ambivalence about, 27–29; prominence of, in three novels, 22
"Gangster as Tragic Hero, The" (Warshow), 28
Gangster film genre, 25, 27–29, 96
Glass Menagerie, The (Williams), 76
God (character, *Summer in Williamsburg*), 51, 52–53, 54, 63, 100, 101–2
Gold, Michael, 19, 48
Grapes of Wrath, The (Steinbeck), 35, 41
Great Gatsby, The (Fitzgerald), 14, 25, 74–75
Grotesques, 17, 36, 50, 52, 76, 98
Group: as character, 88; as hero (in Romains), 39; as protagonist, 35, 39. *See also* Collective protagonist

Halper, Albert, 14, 20
Hammett, Dashiell, 14